# food network magazine

# Best RECIPES 2014

Hearst Editions
New York

# contents

I know exactly where all of my favorite recipes are located, and none of them are in the same place: My pancake recipe is on a Post-it note in the spice cabinet, my go-to cake recipe is on a folded printout next to the cocoa and my favorite weeknight pasta recipe was at one point ripped out of *Food Network Magazine* but is now just in my head. I realize that this is not the best recipe-organizing system (in that it's not organized, or a system), but until recently I didn't have any better ideas. The book you are holding is the answer to my problem: For the first time ever, *Food Network Magazine* editors, along with the chefs in Food Network Kitchens, collected the best recipes of the year and put them in one place. It's such a simple idea, I can't believe we didn't do it sooner.

Choosing the top dishes for this book wasn't easy: The chefs are connected to every recipe they create, and often their ideas are months in the making. As our food director, Liz Sgroi, started narrowing down the list, just for fun she asked the chefs in the test kitchen to name their favorite dish of the year. Three days and many conversations later she still didn't have any answers: "They're my children—I can't pick one," said Katherine Alford, the head of Food Network Kitchens. We didn't let the others off so easy, and after lots of pleading we finally landed on a top five. Vivian Chan, who cross-tests every recipe, picked **Ratatouille Pasta** (page 233). And the developers' picks: Andrea Albin's **Rice Noodle-Shrimp Salad** (page 211); Bob Hoebee's **Shrimp Corn Chowder** (page 34—it's a light version and you'd never know it); Claudia Sidoti's **Shaved Squash and Tomato Pasta** (page 229) and Leah Trent Hope's **Butternut Squash Posole** (page 22). Not that the other 245 recipes aren't also awesome. We picked them carefully to create the ideal mix, virtually guaranteeing that you will never come up short for dinner ideas—and that I will never have to rip apart another issue of the magazine.

*Maile*

Maile Carpenter
Editor in Chief
*Food Network Magazine*

# recipes

## soups & stews

**17** Apple Cheddar Soup with Bacon

**18** Dill Minestrone Soup

**21** Dumpling Soup with Bacon and Snow Peas

**22** Butternut Squash Posole

**25** Chicken and Quinoa Soup

**26** Fresh Tomato Soup with Grilled Cheese

**29** Greek Meatball Stew

**30** Pierogi and Squash Stew

**33** Potato-Fennel Soup

**34** Shrimp Corn Chowder

**37** Summer Vegetable Chili

**38** Chicken Curry Soup

**41** Manhattan Clam Chowder

**42** Slow-Cooker Chili

**Bonus:** Ramen Noodle Soup Bar
**45**

# sandwiches & pizza

**49** French Dip Sandwiches

**50** Ham and Goat Cheese Sandwiches

**53** Three-Cheese Calzones

**54** Cajun Slow-Cooker Pulled Pork

**57** Pesto Chicken Burgers

**58** Chicken Cheesesteaks

**61** Cheesy Cheeseburgers

**62** Tofu Cuban Sandwiches with Jicama Sticks

**65** Ranch Chicken Sandwiches

**66** Beef Pita Pizzas

**Bonus:** Perfect Patties **69**

# poultry

**73** Turkey with Warm Barley Salad

**74** Slow-Cooker Turkey Mole Tacos

**77** Turkey Cobb Salad

**78** Turkey and Quinoa Salad

**81** Turkey Tenders with Cranberry Ketchup

**82** Chili-Rubbed Turkey Cutlets with Black-Eyed Peas

**85** Sloppy Joe Baked Potatoes

**86** Turkey Meatloaf with Sweet Potatoes

**89** Stewed Chicken and Chickpeas

**90** Chicken Cacciatore

**93** Chicken and Chorizo Rice

**94** Chicken Fajitas

**97** Chicken and Rice Casserole

**98** Chicken-Zucchini Chilaquiles

**101** Chipotle Chicken Burritos

**102** Grilled Chicken with Bulgur

**105** Sesame-Lemon Chicken

**106** Roast Chicken with Apple Slaw

**109** Kale-Sesame Chicken Salad

**110** Chicken-Broccoli Stir-Fry

**113** Skillet Chicken and Artichokes

**114** Chicken and Apple Salad

**Bonus:**
Chicken
Breasts
50 Ways
**117**

**Bonus:** Perfect Grilled Steak **179**

**177** Grilled Steak and Vegetables with Lemon-Herb Butter

**174** Chile-Rubbed Steak with Creamed Corn

**173** Steak-Peppercorn Salad

**170** Middle Eastern Steak Pitas

**169** Light Shepherd's Pie

**166** Grilled Cheesy Meatloaves

**165** Skillet Beef Pie

**162** London Broil with Cheesy Yorkshire Pudding

**161** Skirt Steak with Peppers

**158** Asian Steak Frites

**157** Ham and Vegetable Gratin

**154** Stir-Fry Frittata

**153** Bistro Chef's Salad

**150** Pork Tacos with Black Beans

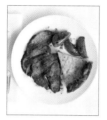

**149** Western Hash Brown Omelet

**146** Pork Tenderloin with Apples

**145** Pork Scallopini Salad

**142** Pork Chops Saltimbocca

**141** Pork and Noodle Stir-Fry

**138** Pork Chops with Pineapple Salsa

**137** Pork Chops with Bean Salad

**134** Mexican Eggs with Chorizo and Beans

**133** Kielbasa with Mashed Potatoes

**130** Hoisin Pork with Rice

**129** Grilled Sausage Kebabs with Pasta Salad

**126** Pork Chops with Corn-Bacon Slaw

**125** Pork with Fennel and Potatoes

**meat**

**Bonus:**
Five
Twists on
Shrimp
Cocktail
**216**

**207** Greek Shrimp and Couscous

**208** Shrimp Francese

**211** Rice Noodle–Shrimp Salad

**212** Spanish Shrimp and Rice

**215** Grilled Beer-and-Butter Shrimp with Potatoes

**195** Roast Cod with Artichokes

**196** Thai Fish Curry

**199** Tuna Salad with Herb Toast

**200** Skillet Orzo with Tuna

**203** Steamed Clams and Kale

**204** Fried Shrimp and Okra

**183** Salmon with Curried Lentils

**184** Buffalo-Style Salmon

**187** Salmon-Apple Burgers

**188** Soy-Maple Salmon

**191** Baked Tilapia with Tomatoes and Potatoes

**192** Blackened Trout with Spicy Kale

# fish & seafood

# pasta & grains

**221** Bucatini with Olive-Caper Sauce

**222** Pasta with Turkey Meatballs

**225** Ham-and-Cheese Noodle Salad

**cover recipe**
**226** Roasted Vegetable Pasta

**229** Shaved Squash and Tomato Pasta

**230** Spaghetti with Pancetta and Chickpeas

**233** Ratatouille Pasta

**234** Spicy Pasta with Tilapia

**237** Broccoli-Cheddar Oven Risotto

**238** Skillet Chicken and Ravioli

**241** Pierogi with Curried Cabbage

**242** Ramen with Pork Meatballs

**245** Cheesy Mushroom Pappardelle

**246** Baked Gnocchi with Chicken

**249** Angel Hair Pasta with Walnut-Carrot Sauce

**Bonus:** Mix & Match Pesto **251**

**Bonus:** 50 Salad Dressings 273

**271** Grapefruit and Poppy Seed Salad

**271** Stir-Fried Broccoli with Cashews

**270** Barley-Leek Pilaf

**269** Fried Zucchini

**268** Spaghetti Squash with Feta

**268** Mexican Honeydew Salad

**267** Grilled Eggplant Salad

**267** Lemon-Herb Orzo

**266** Arugula with Grilled Plums

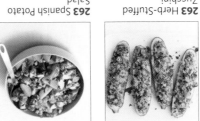

**265** Avocado-Radish Salad

**264** Spicy Wild Rice with Mushrooms

**264** Macaroni and Egg Salad

**263** Spanish Potato Salad

**263** Herb-Stuffed Zucchini

**262** Buttery Beans with Almonds

**261** Wilted Greens with Bacon

**260** Tex-Mex Salad

**260** Edamame with Bacon

**259** Carrot-Cashew Salad

**259** Pomegranate-Glazed Squash

**258** Smoky Roasted Mushrooms

**257** Chard, Squash and Tomatoes

**256** Roasted Brussels Sprouts and Carrots

**256** Winter Caprese Salad

**255** Whipped Parsnips

**255** Spicy Watercress with Ginger

**254** Spiced Oven-Fried Potatoes

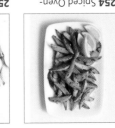

# side dishes

# cookies

**284** Pumpkin Thumbprints

**285** Amaretto Biscotti

**286** Chocolate-Orange Crackles

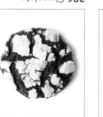

**287** Glazed Cider Cookies

**288** Chewy Oatmeal-Cranberry Cookies

**289** Lemon-Rosemary Macaroons

**278** Linzer Bars

**279** Lemon-Ginger Wafers

**280** Blood Orange Macaroons

**281** Cocoa Palmiers

**282** Peanut Butter Brownie Bites

**283** Salted Caramel Shortbread

# soups & stews

# APPLE-CHEDDAR SOUP WITH BACON

ACTIVE: 30 min | TOTAL: 40 min | SERVES: 4

| | |
|---|---|
| 3 | slices bacon |
| 1 | small onion, chopped |
| 2 | medium apples, peeled and chopped |
| 1 | medium potato, peeled and chopped |
| 3 | cups low-sodium chicken broth |
| 1½ | cups unsweetened apple juice |
| | Kosher salt and freshly ground pepper |
| 2 | cups shredded extra-sharp cheddar cheese (about 8 ounces) |
| 2 | slices rye bread, toasted |
| 2 | teaspoons dijon mustard |
| | Chopped fresh chives, for topping |

**1.** Cook the bacon in a large pot over medium heat until crisp, 4 to 5 minutes per side. Transfer to paper towels to drain; let cool slightly, then roughly chop. Pour out all but 2 tablespoons of the drippings from the pot.

**2.** Increase the heat under the pot to medium high. Add the onion, apples and potato and cook, stirring frequently, until the apples are soft, about 8 minutes. Add the chicken broth, apple juice, ¾ teaspoon salt, and pepper to taste. Bring to a simmer and cook until the potato is soft, 10 to 12 minutes. Stir in all but 2 tablespoons of the cheddar until melted. Working in batches, transfer the soup to a blender and puree. Return to the pot and season with salt and pepper.

**3.** Meanwhile, preheat the broiler. Spread the bread with the mustard and sprinkle with the reserved 2 tablespoons cheese. Broil until the cheese melts, about 30 seconds, then cut into 1-inch squares. Ladle the soup into bowls and top with the bacon, chives, cheese croutons and more pepper.

Per serving: Calories 492; Fat 29 g (Saturated 15 g); Cholesterol 89 mg; Sodium 1,098 mg; Carbohydrate 36 g; Fiber 4 g; Protein 23 g

# DILL MINESTRONE SOUP

ACTIVE: 25 min | TOTAL: 40 min | SERVES: 4

LOW-CALORIE DINNER

Kosher salt

| | |
|---|---|
| 1 | cup small pasta shells |
| 2 | tablespoons extra-virgin olive oil, plus more for drizzling |
| 1 | medium onion, finely chopped |
| 4 | ounces Canadian bacon, finely chopped |
| 2 | cloves garlic, finely chopped |
| 1 | teaspoon Worcestershire sauce |
| ⅓ | cup chopped fresh dill |
| 8 | cups precut mixed vegetables |
| 4 | cups low-sodium chicken broth |
| | Freshly ground pepper |
| ⅓ | cup sour cream |
| | Paprika, for topping |
| | Whole-wheat rolls, for serving (optional) |

**1.** Bring a large pot of salted water to a boil. Add the pasta and cook as the label directs, then drain and rinse under cold water. Transfer to a bowl; drizzle lightly with olive oil and set aside.

**2.** Meanwhile, heat 2 tablespoons olive oil in a large pot over medium-high heat. Add the onion, Canadian bacon, garlic, Worcestershire sauce and half of the dill and cook, stirring occasionally, until the onion is soft and slightly golden, 6 to 8 minutes.

**3.** Add the mixed vegetables and ¼ cup water to the pot; cover and cook until beginning to soften, 4 minutes. Add the broth, 2 cups water, 1 teaspoon salt, and pepper to taste. Bring to a high simmer and cook, uncovered, until the vegetables are tender, 12 to 15 more minutes. Stir in the pasta and the remaining dill; season with salt and pepper.

**4.** Divide the soup among bowls. Top with the sour cream and sprinkle with paprika. Serve with rolls.

Per serving: Calories 403; Fat 15 g (Saturated 5 g); Cholesterol 53 mg; Sodium 1,145 mg; Carbohydrate 47 g; Fiber 9 g; Protein 21 g

# DUMPLING SOUP WITH BACON AND SNOW PEAS

ACTIVE: 15 min | TOTAL: 25 min | SERVES: 4

4   slices thick-cut bacon, cut into ½-inch pieces
2   tablespoons minced peeled ginger
1   bunch scallions, chopped
    Kosher salt
1   teaspoon sugar
4   cups low-sodium chicken broth
2   tablespoons cornstarch
2   tablespoons sesame oil
    Freshly ground pepper
4   ounces snow peas, trimmed and cut into 1-inch pieces
2   plum tomatoes, cut into 1-inch pieces
1   bunch watercress, tough stems trimmed, cut into 2-inch pieces
1   pound frozen Asian-style dumplings or pot stickers

**1.** Cook the bacon in a Dutch oven or large pot over medium-high heat until browned around the edges, about 5 minutes. Add the ginger, half of the scallions, 1 teaspoon salt and the sugar; stir-fry 30 seconds. Add the broth and 1 cup water; cover and bring to a boil. Meanwhile, combine the cornstarch and 3 tablespoons water in a small bowl. Add the sesame oil and 1 teaspoon pepper and stir to combine.

**2.** Add the snow peas, tomatoes, watercress and dumplings to the boiling broth mixture. Stir the cornstarch mixture again and add to the soup. Cook, stirring occasionally, until the dumplings are tender and the broth thickens slightly, 3 to 5 minutes. Stir in the remaining scallions and season with pepper.

Per serving: Calories 430; Fat 22 g (Saturated 6 g); Cholesterol 65 mg; Sodium 1,337 mg; Carbohydrate 38 g; Fiber 3 g; Protein 22 g

DONE IN 25 MINUTES

# BUTTERNUT SQUASH POSOLE

ACTIVE: 30 min | TOTAL: 40 min | SERVES: 4

**LOW-CALORIE DINNER**

| 2 | tablespoons vegetable oil |
| 1 | tablespoon chili powder |
| 1 | small butternut squash, peeled, seeded and cut into ¾-inch cubes (about 4 cups) |
| 1 | poblano chile pepper, seeded and chopped |
| 1 | teaspoon dried oregano, plus more for sprinkling |
| 1 | teaspoon ground cumin |
| 2 | cloves garlic, finely chopped |
| | Kosher salt |
| 1 | 15-ounce can no-salt-added tomato puree |
| 2 | 15-ounce cans hominy, drained and rinsed |
| 1 | avocado, diced |
| | Fresh salsa, for topping (optional) |
| | Tortilla chips, for serving (optional) |

**1.** Heat the vegetable oil in a large Dutch oven or heavy-bottomed pot over medium-high heat. Stir in the chili powder. Add the squash, poblano, oregano, cumin, garlic and ½ teaspoon salt and cook, stirring frequently, until the poblano softens slightly, about 5 minutes. Add 5 cups water, the tomato puree and ½ teaspoon salt; cover and bring to a simmer. Uncover and cook until the squash is tender, about 15 minutes, adding the hominy during the last 2 minutes of cooking.

**2.** Season the posole with salt and divide among bowls. Top with the avocado and salsa and sprinkle with oregano. Serve with chips.

Per serving: Calories 415; Fat 16 g (Saturated 2 g); Cholesterol 0 mg; Sodium 1,451 mg; Carbohydrate 76 g; Fiber 17 g; Protein 9 g

# CHICKEN AND QUINOA SOUP

ACTIVE: 15 min I TOTAL: 35 min I SERVES: 4

LOW-CALORIE DINNER

| | |
|---|---|
| 1 | tablespoon extra-virgin olive oil |
| 1 | medium onion, sliced |
| 3 | stalks celery, chopped |
| 2 | cups roughly chopped carrots |
| 1 | teaspoon Cajun seasoning, plus more for topping |
| 1 | cup quinoa |
| 1 | quart fat-free low-sodium chicken broth |

Kosher salt and freshly ground pepper

| | |
|---|---|
| 2 | cups chopped broccoli florets |
| 2½ | cups shredded rotisserie chicken (white meat only), skin removed |
| 2 | tablespoons low-fat sour cream |

**1.** Heat the olive oil in a large pot over medium-high heat. Add the onion, celery, carrots and Cajun seasoning and cook, stirring occasionally, until the vegetables are slightly soft, about 4 minutes.

**2.** Stir in the quinoa, then add the chicken broth, 3 cups water, ½ teaspoon salt, and pepper to taste. Partially cover and bring to a simmer, then reduce the heat to medium and cook until the quinoa starts to soften, about 12 minutes. Add the broccoli and cook, uncovered, until just tender, about 5 minutes. Add the chicken and stir to warm through. Season with salt and pepper.

**3.** Ladle the soup into bowls. Top with the sour cream and Cajun seasoning to taste.

Per serving: Calories 436; Fat 11 g (Saturated 2 g); Cholesterol 88 mg; Sodium 1,441 mg; Carbohydrate 45 g; Fiber 6 g; Protein 43 g

LOW-CALORIE DINNER

# FRESH TOMATO SOUP WITH GRILLED CHEESE

ACTIVE: 30 min I TOTAL: 35 min I SERVES: 4

4½  pounds tomatoes (4 pounds quartered, ½ pound chopped)
2    tablespoons extra-virgin olive oil
1    clove garlic, minced
4    scallions, chopped
1½  tablespoons heavy cream
Kosher salt and freshly ground pepper
½    cup mini bow ties or other mini pasta
½    cup shredded part-skim mozzarella cheese
½    cup shredded sharp cheddar cheese
4    slices multigrain bread
2    thin slices low-sodium ham
Chopped fresh basil, for topping

**1.** Puree the quartered tomatoes in a blender. Heat 1½ tablespoons olive oil in a pot over medium heat. Add the garlic and half of the scallions and cook, stirring, 2 minutes. Increase the heat to medium high; strain the pureed tomatoes through a mesh sieve into the pot. Stir in the chopped tomatoes, 1 cup water, the cream, ½ teaspoon salt and ¼ teaspoon pepper. Bring to a simmer and cook until thickened, about 5 minutes. Add the pasta and cook until tender, about 10 minutes; season with salt and pepper.
**2.** Toss the remaining scallions with the cheeses; divide half the mixture between 2 bread slices. Top each with a slice of ham, the remaining cheese mixture and the other 2 bread slices. Heat the remaining ½ tablespoon olive oil in a nonstick skillet over medium-low heat. Cook the sandwiches until the cheese melts, 3 minutes per side; cut in half. Ladle the soup into bowls; top with basil and serve with the sandwiches.

Per serving: Calories 418; Fat 20 g (Saturated 7 g); Cholesterol 36 mg; Sodium 682 mg; Carbohydrate 44 g; Fiber 8 g; Protein 18 g

LOW-CALORIE DINNER

# GREEK MEATBALL STEW
ACTIVE: 20 min **I** TOTAL: 30 min **I** SERVES: 4

| | |
|---|---|
| 2 | cups low-sodium chicken broth |
| 2 | 14-ounce cans diced fire-roasted tomatoes with green chiles |
| 1 | large red onion, cut into chunks |
| 1 | cup pimiento-stuffed green olives |
| 1 | cup lightly packed fresh mint, dill or a combination |
| 1 | teaspoon dried oregano |
| ½ | teaspoon ground pumpkin pie spice or allspice |
| 2 | thick slices sandwich bread, torn into pieces |
| 12 | ounces ground beef chuck |
| 1 | 14-ounce can butter beans, drained and rinsed |
| 1 | large or 2 small zucchini, quartered lengthwise and cut into ½-inch pieces |

Juice of 1 lemon

**1.** Put the chicken broth and tomatoes in a large Dutch oven or pot, cover and bring to a boil over medium-high heat. Meanwhile, put the onion, olives, mint, oregano and pumpkin pie spice in a food processor; pulse until very finely chopped. Add half of the onion mixture to the pot.

**2.** Add the bread to the food processor with the remaining onion mixture and pulse to form wet crumbs. Transfer to a large bowl, add the beef and mix with your hands until just combined. Form into 20 small meatballs and add to the pot. Cook, turning the meatballs once, until just firm, about 3 minutes.

**3.** Gently stir the butter beans and zucchini into the stew; cook until the zucchini is tender, about 5 minutes. Add lemon juice to taste.

Per serving: Calories 436; Fat 20 g (Saturated 8 g); Cholesterol 60 mg; Sodium 1,294 mg; Carbohydrate 43 g; Fiber 8 g; Protein 26 g

# PIEROGI AND SQUASH STEW

ACTIVE: 25 min I TOTAL: 35 min I SERVES: 4

LOW-
CALORIE
DINNER

| | |
|---|---|
| 2 | teaspoons extra-virgin olive oil |
| 8 | ounces Italian turkey sausage, casings removed |
| 1 | tablespoon tomato paste |
| 1 | pound cremini mushrooms, sliced |
| 2 | tablespoons all-purpose flour |
| 2 | cups low-sodium chicken broth |
| 3 | cups shredded coleslaw mix or shredded cabbage |
| 1 | 10-ounce bag frozen cubed butternut squash, thawed |
| 1 | 12-to-13-ounce package cheddar and potato pierogies |

Kosher salt
⅓   cup sour cream
Freshly ground pepper

**1.** Heat the olive oil in a large pot over medium heat; add the sausage and cook, breaking it up with a wooden spoon, until browned, about 5 minutes. Add the tomato paste and cook, stirring, 30 seconds. Add the mushrooms and stir well to coat. Increase the heat to medium high, cover and cook, stirring occasionally, until the mushrooms are tender, about 5 minutes. Add the flour and cook, stirring, 1 minute, then stir in the chicken broth and 2 cups water, scraping up any browned bits from the bottom of the pot.
**2.** Add the coleslaw mix to the pot, cover and bring to a simmer. Reduce the heat to medium and cook until the cabbage is wilted, about 3 minutes. Add the squash and pierogies and simmer, uncovered, until the pierogies are cooked through, 5 to 7 minutes. Season with salt. Divide among bowls and top with the sour cream, and pepper to taste.

Per serving: Calories 388; Fat 13 g (Saturated 5 g); Cholesterol 75 mg; Sodium 763 mg; Carbohydrate 46 g; Fiber 4 g; Protein 24 g

## POTATO-FENNEL SOUP

ACTIVE: 30 min **I** TOTAL: 40 min **I** SERVES: 4

3    large leeks
1    large bulb fennel, diced (stems and fronds reserved)
3    large carrots, diced
Kosher salt and freshly ground pepper
Cooking spray
2    tablespoons unsalted butter
2    pounds Yukon gold potatoes, peeled and cut into 1-inch pieces
1½   cups skim milk
¼    cup chopped fresh parsley and/or dill
½    cup low-fat ricotta cheese
4    slices crusty Italian bread, toasted

**1.** Preheat the oven to 450°. Make the broth: Cut off the dark green tops of the leeks and put in a large pot along with the fennel stems and fronds; add 8 cups water. Bring to a boil, then reduce the heat to medium, cover and simmer 20 minutes.
**2.** Meanwhile, halve the remaining leeks lengthwise, then thinly slice and rinse. Put the carrots and half each of the sliced leeks and diced fennel on a foil-lined baking sheet. Season with salt and pepper, coat with cooking spray and toss. Roast until golden, about 25 minutes.
**3.** Meanwhile, melt the butter in a Dutch oven or pot over medium-high heat. Add the remaining leeks and fennel and cook, stirring, until soft, about 4 minutes. Add the potatoes and 2 cups of the prepared broth. Cover and cook until tender, 15 minutes. Add 4 more cups broth and the milk; bring to a boil. Working in batches, transfer to a blender and puree; season with salt and pepper.
**4.** Ladle the soup into bowls; top with the roasted vegetables and chopped herbs. Spread the ricotta on the toasted bread and season with pepper; serve with the soup.

Per serving: Calories 476; Fat 9 g (Saturated 5 g); Cholesterol 26 mg; Sodium 306 mg; Carbohydrate 82 g; Fiber 9 g; Protein 17 g

# SHRIMP CORN CHOWDER

ACTIVE: 20 min I TOTAL: 30 min I SERVES: 4

| | |
|---|---|
| 2 | teaspoons unsalted butter |
| 3 | stalks celery, thinly sliced |
| 2 | bunches scallions, chopped |
| 3 | cups frozen diced potatoes |
| 3 | cups frozen corn |
| 3 | sprigs thyme |
| 2 | bay leaves |

Kosher salt and freshly ground pepper

| | |
|---|---|
| 2 | tablespoons all-purpose flour |
| 1 | quart low-fat milk |
| 1 | pound medium shrimp, peeled and deveined |

Paprika, for sprinkling

**1.** Melt the butter in a Dutch oven or large pot over medium-high heat. Stir in the celery, scallions, potatoes and corn. Add the thyme, bay leaves, ½ teaspoon salt and a few grinds of pepper and cook, stirring, 3 minutes. Stir in the flour until incorporated, about 2 minutes. Stir in the milk, then cover and bring to a boil. Uncover, reduce the heat to medium low and gently simmer until the vegetables are tender, about 6 minutes. Remove from the heat. Discard the thyme sprigs and bay leaves.

**2.** Transfer one-third of the mixture to a blender and puree until smooth, then return to the pot. Return to a simmer over medium-high heat. Stir in the shrimp and cook until opaque, about 4 minutes. Season with salt. If the soup is too thick, stir in up to 1 cup water. Divide among bowls and sprinkle with paprika.

Per serving: Calories 394; Fat 8 g (Saturated 5 g); Cholesterol 193 mg; Sodium 658 mg; Carbohydrate 49 g; Fiber 8 g; Protein 32 g

## SUMMER VEGETABLE CHILI
ACTIVE: 25 min  I  TOTAL: 40 min  I  SERVES: 4

| | |
|---|---|
| 3 | tablespoons vegetable oil |
| 1 | medium red onion, chopped |
| 3 | cloves garlic, chopped |
| 2 | tablespoons chili powder |
| 2 | teaspoons ground cumin |
| 1 | poblano chile pepper, seeded and diced |
| 2 | portobello mushrooms, stemmed and chopped |
| 2 | cups frozen corn (preferably fire-roasted), thawed |
| 2 | 14-ounce cans no-salt-added pinto beans |
| 1 | 14-ounce can no-salt-added diced tomatoes |

Kosher salt and freshly ground pepper
Shredded cheddar cheese, sour cream and/or torn fresh cilantro, for topping
(optional)
8    corn tortillas, warmed

**1.** Heat the vegetable oil in a large pot over medium heat. Add all but a few tablespoons of the chopped red onion. Stir in the garlic, chili powder and cumin and cook, stirring occasionally, until the onion begins to soften, about 3 minutes. Add the poblano, mushrooms and corn and cook, stirring occasionally, until just tender, about 3 more minutes. Add the beans, tomatoes, 1½ cups water and ½ teaspoon each salt and pepper. Bring to a boil, then stir and reduce the heat to medium. Simmer, stirring occasionally, until the vegetables are tender and the chili is thick, about 20 minutes. Season with salt and pepper.
**2.** Divide the chili among bowls. Top with the cheese, sour cream and/or cilantro; sprinkle with the reserved red onion. Serve with the tortillas.

Per serving: Calories 504; Fat 13 g (Saturated 1 g); Cholesterol 0 mg;
Sodium 421 mg; Carbohydrate 79 g; Fiber 16 g; Protein 16 g

## CHICKEN CURRY SOUP
ACTIVE: 20 min **I** TOTAL: 40 min **I** SERVES: 4

1    bunch scallions (white and light green parts only), chopped
1    jalapeño pepper, seeded and roughly chopped
2    ¼-inch-thick slices peeled ginger
½    cup cilantro, plus more for topping
4    cloves garlic
3    cooking apples (such as McIntosh or Fuji),
     peeled and roughly chopped
2    teaspoons curry powder
1    13.5-ounce can light coconut milk
Kosher salt
4    cups low-sodium chicken broth
1    cup red lentils, picked over and rinsed
½    pound skinless, boneless chicken breasts,
     cut into ¾-inch pieces
Freshly ground pepper

**1.** Pulse the scallions, jalapeño, ginger, cilantro and garlic in a food processor until chopped. With the motor running, add the apples, a few pieces at a time, until chopped.
**2.** Cook the curry powder in a Dutch oven or large pot over medium-high heat, stirring, until lightly toasted, about 1 minute. Whisk in the coconut milk until smooth; cook until reduced by half, about 5 minutes. Add the apple-scallion mixture and ½ teaspoon salt. Cook, stirring, until thickened, about 5 more minutes.
**3.** Stir in the chicken broth and lentils. Bring to a boil, then reduce the heat to medium low and simmer until the lentils are tender and broken down, about 15 minutes. Add the chicken and simmer until cooked through, about 6 minutes. Season with salt and pepper; top with cilantro.

Per serving: Calories 399; Fat 9 g (Saturated 6 g); Cholesterol 58 mg; Sodium 446 mg; Carbohydrate 50 g; Fiber 11 g; Protein 34 g

# MANHATTAN CLAM CHOWDER

ACTIVE: 20 min **I** TOTAL: 40 min **I** SERVES: 4

LOW-CALORIE DINNER

3   slices thick-cut bacon, cut into ½-inch pieces
4   stalks celery, thinly sliced
3   medium Yukon gold potatoes (about 1 pound),
    peeled and cut into ¾-inch pieces
1   large onion, finely chopped
1   large carrot, cut into ½-inch pieces
1   clove garlic, minced
2   bay leaves
6   sprigs thyme, leaves coarsely chopped
Kosher salt and freshly ground pepper
1   28-ounce can crushed San Marzano tomatoes
1   1-pound package frozen shelled clams, thawed
2   cups bottled clam juice
Oyster crackers, for serving (optional)

**1.** Cook the bacon in a Dutch oven or large pot over medium-high heat, stirring occasionally, until slightly browned, about 3 minutes. Add the celery, potatoes, onion, carrot, garlic, bay leaves, thyme, 1 teaspoon salt and ½ teaspoon pepper. Cook, stirring occasionally, until the celery and onion begin to soften, about 3 minutes.
**2.** Add the tomatoes to the pot and cook 2 minutes. Add the clams and their juices, 1 cup water and the bottled clam juice; cover and bring to a boil. Reduce the heat to medium and simmer, covered, until the potatoes are tender, 20 to 25 minutes. Season with salt and pepper. Serve with oyster crackers.

Per serving: Calories 408; Fat 17 g (Saturated 6 g); Cholesterol 65 mg; Sodium 1,184 mg; Carbohydrate 39 g; Fiber 6 g; Protein 24 g

LOW-CALORIE DINNER

# SLOW-COOKER CHILI

ACTIVE: 10 min I TOTAL: 10 min (plus 8-hr slow cooking) I SERVES: 8

¼   cup tomato paste
½   cup brewed coffee
2   pounds beef chuck, cut into 1½-inch pieces
1   tablespoon chili powder
Kosher salt and freshly ground pepper
2   15-ounce cans pinto beans (do not drain)
½   cup crushed tortilla chips
4   cups cooked white rice
Shredded cheddar cheese, sliced scallions and
    diced avocado, for topping (optional)

**1.** Mix the tomato paste and coffee in a small bowl; set aside. Toss the meat with the chili powder, 1½ teaspoons salt and ¼ teaspoon pepper in a 6-quart slow cooker. Stir in the beans (with their liquid), the coffee mixture and the tortilla chips.
**2.** Cover the slow cooker and cook on low until the beef is tender, 8 hours. Season with salt. Serve the chili with the rice; top with cheese, scallions and avocado.

Per serving: Calories 414; Fat 14 g (Saturated 5 g); Cholesterol 75 mg; Sodium 719 mg; Carbohydrate 40 g; Fiber 7 g; Protein 30 g

# Top This

# RAMEN NOODLE SOUP

ACTIVE: 45 min **I** TOTAL: 2 hr **I** SERVES: 8

¼  cup vegetable oil
8  cloves garlic, smashed
1  large onion, chopped
8  thin slices ginger
1  pound sliced bacon
4  pounds chicken wings
12  dried shiitake mushrooms, rinsed
12  scallions, white and light green parts, chopped
¼  cup sake or dry sherry
¼  cup reduced-sodium soy sauce
Kosher salt
1  teaspoon sugar
1  teaspoon white peppercorns
8  3-to-5-ounce packages dry or vacuum-packed ramen noodles (flavor packets discarded)
Assorted toppings (at right)

**1.** Heat 3 tablespoons vegetable oil in a large skillet over medium heat. Add the garlic, onion and ginger and cook, stirring occasionally, until the onion is dark brown, about 30 minutes.
**2.** Meanwhile, make the broth: Put the bacon and chicken wings in a Dutch oven and add enough water to cover. Bring to a boil, then reduce the heat to medium and simmer 10 minutes. Drain and wipe the pot clean. Rinse the bacon and wings under cold water, then return to the pot; add 4 quarts water and the dried mushrooms. Bring to a boil, then reduce the heat to medium; add the garlic mixture and gently simmer 1 hour, 15 minutes.
**3.** Strain the broth through a colander into a large bowl, pressing on the solids to extract as much of the liquid as possible. Skim any excess fat from the surface. Measure the broth, adding water, if necessary, to yield 2 quarts. (The broth can be made up to 4 days ahead; cover and refrigerate.)
**4.** Just before serving, heat the remaining 1 tablespoon vegetable oil and the scallions in a medium skillet over medium heat until the mixture starts sizzling. Add the sake, soy sauce, 1½ teaspoons salt, the sugar, peppercorns and ½ cup water. Simmer, reducing to ½ cup, about 5 minutes.
**5.** Bring the broth and the scallion mixture to a simmer in a large saucepan over medium heat. Add the noodles and cook until softened, 1 to 3 minutes. Gently pull the noodles apart with tongs. Transfer the soup to bowls and top as desired.

## TOPPINGS BAR
Take your pick: These taste great in just about any combination.

Shredded rotisserie chicken

Sautéed mushrooms

Nori strips (seaweed)

Shredded kale

Cubed firm tofu

Snow peas

Toasted sesame seeds

Sliced radishes

Sliced scallions

Bean sprouts

Kimchi

Watercress

Sliced jalapeño

Pickled ginger

Wasabi paste

Fried egg

Sesame oil

Sriracha

Roasted squash
Toss cubed butternut or kabocha squash (no need to peel) with olive oil and sprinkle with salt, sugar and red pepper flakes. Roast at 425°, 30 minutes.

Sautéed shrimp
Stir-fry peeled deveined shrimp in hot olive oil with minced ginger, chopped scallions and a pinch each of sugar, salt and pepper.

Roasted pork belly
Put 1 cup each sake and water, ½ cup each soy sauce and mirin, and ¼ cup sugar in a Dutch oven. Add 2 pounds skinless pork belly, 1 quartered onion, ½ head garlic and 4 thin slices ginger. Cover with foil. Roast at 325°, 3 hours; slice.

# sandwiches
# &pizza

# FRENCH DIP SANDWICHES

ACTIVE: 35 min **I** TOTAL: 35 min **I** SERVES: 4

3½  tablespoons unsalted butter
1  large onion, thinly sliced
Kosher salt
1½  cups low-sodium beef broth
¼  teaspoon freshly grated nutmeg
1  tablespoon horseradish, plus more to taste
8  ounces gruyère cheese, thinly sliced
¾  pound thinly sliced roast beef
4  hoagie rolls, split

**1.** Melt 1 tablespoon butter in a large nonstick skillet over medium-high heat. Add the onion and ¼ teaspoon salt; cook, stirring, until golden brown, about 10 minutes. Transfer to a bowl; reserve the skillet.
**2.** Meanwhile, make the dip: Bring the beef broth and nutmeg to a simmer in a small saucepan; remove from the heat and add the horseradish and ½ tablespoon butter. Cover and keep warm.
**3.** Layer half of the cheese, then the roast beef, onion and the remaining cheese on the rolls. Melt 1 tablespoon butter in the skillet over medium heat. Add 2 sandwiches and top with a heavy skillet. Cook, pressing down on the top skillet to flatten the sandwiches, until the bread is golden brown and the cheese melts, about 4 minutes per side. Repeat with the remaining 1 tablespoon butter and 2 sandwiches. Serve with the dip.

Per serving: Calories 675; Fat 37 g (Saturated 20 g); Cholesterol 142 mg; Sodium 989 mg; Carbohydrate 39 g; Fiber 3 g; Protein 46 g

DONE IN
10
MINUTES

# HAM AND GOAT CHEESE SANDWICHES

ACTIVE: 10 min I TOTAL: 10 min I SERVES: 4

6    ounces goat cheese
3    tablespoons pepitas (hulled green pumpkin seeds) or chopped almonds
Chipotle hot sauce
8    slices whole-grain sandwich bread, toasted
½    pound thinly sliced Black Forest ham
1    avocado, pitted, peeled and sliced
2    cups baby arugula or mixed baby greens
2    teaspoons extra-virgin olive oil
Kosher salt and freshly ground pepper
Potato salad, for serving (optional)

1. Mash the goat cheese, pepitas and 2 to 3 teaspoons hot sauce in a bowl with a fork until combined. Spread the mixture evenly on 4 slices of bread, then top with the ham and avocado.
2. Toss the arugula with the olive oil, a few dashes of hot sauce, and salt and pepper to taste in a bowl. Add the arugula to the sandwiches and cover with the remaining bread. Serve with potato salad.

Per serving: Calories 479; Fat 30 g (Saturated 9 g); Cholesterol 41 mg; Sodium 1,088 mg; Carbohydrate 38 g; Fiber 10 g; Protein 27 g

## THREE-CHEESE CALZONES
ACTIVE: 25 min I TOTAL: 40 min I SERVES: 4

| | |
|---|---|
| 2 | cups shredded part-skim mozzarella cheese (about 8 ounces) |
| ½ | cup ricotta cheese |
| ½ | cup fresh basil, chopped |
| 2 | scallions, sliced |
| ¼ | cup plus 2 teaspoons grated parmesan cheese (about 1½ ounces) |
| 1 | tablespoon breadcrumbs |
| 1 | pound prepared pizza dough, at room temperature |

All-purpose flour, for dusting
1    large egg, lightly beaten
Marinara sauce, warmed, for dipping
4    ounces sliced salami
Giardiniera (Italian pickled vegetables), for serving (optional)

1. Preheat the oven to 450°. Line a baking sheet with foil.
2. Make the filling: Mix the mozzarella, ricotta, basil, scallions, ¼ cup parmesan and the breadcrumbs in a medium bowl until combined. Divide the pizza dough into 4 equal pieces. Roll out each piece on a lightly floured surface into a 7-to-8-inch round.
3. Spoon one-quarter of the filling onto one half of each dough round, leaving a ½-inch border. Lightly brush the edges of the dough with some of the beaten egg; fold the dough over the filling and crimp the edges with a fork to seal. Transfer the calzones to the prepared baking sheet.
4. Brush the calzones with the remaining beaten egg and cut 2 slits in the top of each to let steam escape. Sprinkle the calzones with the remaining 2 teaspoons parmesan, then bake until golden brown and cooked through, 18 to 20 minutes. Serve with marinara sauce, the salami and giardiniera.

Per serving: Calories 725; Fat 39 g (Saturated 17 g); Cholesterol 141 mg;
Sodium 1,432 mg; Carbohydrate 61 g; Fiber 3 g; Protein 38 g

## CAJUN SLOW-COOKER PULLED PORK

ACTIVE: 20 min **I** TOTAL: 30 min (plus 8-hr slow cooking) **I** SERVES: 8

| | |
|---|---|
| ½ | cup apple cider vinegar |
| ⅓ | cup ketchup |
| ¼ | cup plus 2 tablespoons Creole or spicy brown mustard |
| 1 | tablespoon molasses |
| 2 | tablespoons packed light brown sugar |
| 2 | teaspoons paprika |

Kosher salt and freshly ground pepper

| | |
|---|---|
| 1 | 3-to-4-pound boneless pork shoulder |
| 2 | links andouille sausage |
| ⅓ | cup mayonnaise |
| 8 | soft sesame buns |

Pickle slices and potato chips, for serving (optional)

1. Whisk 1½ cups water, the vinegar, ketchup, ¼ cup mustard, the molasses and 1 tablespoon brown sugar in a 7-to-8-quart slow cooker.
2. Combine the remaining 1 tablespoon brown sugar, the paprika, 1 teaspoon salt and ½ teaspoon pepper in a small bowl. Rub all over the pork, then add to the slow cooker along with the sausage. Cover and cook on low, 8 hours.
3. Remove the pork and sausage and set aside to cool slightly. Skim off the excess fat from the cooking liquid, then strain into a large skillet and bring to a boil. Cook until reduced by one-third, about 15 minutes.
4. Shred the pork with a fork and coarsely chop the sausage. Toss the pork and sausage with enough of the reduced cooking liquid to moisten; season with salt.
5. Whisk the mayonnaise and the remaining 2 tablespoons mustard in a small bowl; spread on the buns. Fill with the pulled pork and pickle slices. Serve with potato chips.

Per serving: Calories 533; Fat 29 g (Saturated 9 g); Cholesterol 157 mg; Sodium 1,094 mg; Carbohydrate 23 g; Fiber 1 g; Protein 43 g

## PESTO CHICKEN BURGERS

ACTIVE: 35 min I TOTAL: 35 min I SERVES: 4

5   whole-wheat hamburger buns (1 cut into pieces, 4 split open and toasted)
1¼  pounds ground chicken
Kosher salt and freshly ground pepper
2   tablespoons extra-virgin olive oil
3   tablespoons sliced almonds
2   medium tomatoes (1 whole, 1 thickly sliced)
4   cups loosely packed fresh basil (about 1 bunch)
2   tablespoons grated parmesan cheese
1   5-ounce package baby arugula
Juice of ½ lemon

1. Toss the cut-up bun with 3 tablespoons water in a large bowl; set aside 1 minute. Add the chicken, ¾ teaspoon salt, and pepper to taste; mix with your hands until combined. Form into four ¾-inch-thick patties.

2. Heat the olive oil in a large nonstick skillet over medium heat. Add the almonds and cook, stirring, until lightly toasted, about 2 minutes. Set aside 1 tablespoon almonds for the salad; transfer the rest to a blender along with the oil from the pan. Do not wipe out the skillet.

3. Increase the heat under the skillet to medium high. Add the chicken patties and cook until no longer pink, 7 to 8 minutes per side.

4. Meanwhile, add the whole tomato to the blender and process until smooth. Add the basil and ¼ teaspoon salt; pulse until almost smooth. Add the parmesan; pulse until combined. Season with salt and pepper.

5. Serve the burgers on the buns; top each with a spoonful of pesto and a tomato slice. Toss the remaining pesto with the arugula, the reserved 1 tablespoon almonds and the lemon juice; serve with the burgers.

Per serving: Calories 469; Fat 25 g (Saturated 6 g); Cholesterol 99 mg; Sodium 763 mg; Carbohydrate 34 g; Fiber 6 g; Protein 31 g

## CHICKEN CHEESESTEAKS
ACTIVE: 30 min I TOTAL: 30 min I SERVES: 4

1½   pounds skinless, boneless chicken thighs
3   tablespoons extra-virgin olive oil
½   teaspoon paprika
Kosher salt and freshly ground pepper
1   large onion, thinly sliced
2   cloves garlic, finely chopped
½   cup pickled sweet or hot cherry peppers, sliced
4   soft hoagie rolls, split
6   slices American cheese (about 4½ ounces), halved
Hot sauce and/or ketchup, for topping (optional)
Carrot and celery sticks, for serving (optional)

1. Preheat the oven to 450°. Line a baking sheet with foil. Toss the chicken, 1 tablespoon olive oil, the paprika, ½ teaspoon salt and ¼ teaspoon pepper in a bowl; spread in a single layer on the baking sheet. Roast until just cooked through, 15 minutes. Transfer the chicken to a cutting board; discard the foil and reserve the baking sheet.

2. Heat 1 tablespoon olive oil in a skillet over medium-high heat; add the onion and cook, stirring occasionally, until golden, 6 to 8 minutes. Add the garlic, ¼ teaspoon salt, and pepper to taste and cook, 1 minute. Remove from the heat and stir in the pickled peppers.

3. Brush the insides of the rolls with the remaining 1 tablespoon olive oil; arrange cut-side up on the baking sheet and toast in the oven, about 2 minutes. Thinly slice the chicken and divide among the rolls. Top evenly with the onion mixture and the cheese. Return to the oven to melt the cheese, about 2 minutes. Top with hot sauce and/or ketchup and serve with carrot and celery sticks.

Per serving: Calories 625; Fat 30 g (Saturated 9 g); Cholesterol 166 mg; Sodium 1,248 mg; Carbohydrate 41 g; Fiber 3 g; Protein 46 g

## CHEESY CHEESEBURGERS
ACTIVE: 20 min **I** TOTAL: 20 min **I** SERVES: 4

DONE IN
20
MINUTES

1½  pounds ground beef chuck
4  ½-inch cubes pepper jack cheese (about 1 ounce total)
Kosher salt and freshly ground pepper
½  tablespoon vegetable oil
4  slices cheddar cheese (about 2 ounces)
4  hamburger buns
Ketchup, mustard and/or mayonnaise, for spreading
Lettuce leaves, sliced tomato and/or sliced red onion, for topping
Pickles, for serving (optional)

**1.** Divide the beef into 4 equal portions. Press a cube of pepper jack into the center of each and shape the meat around the cheese; form into patties, about 4 inches wide and ¾ inch thick. Season the patties with salt and pepper.
**2.** Heat the vegetable oil in a large skillet over medium-high heat. Add the patties and cook until browned on the bottom, about 4 minutes. Flip the patties and top each with a slice of cheddar; cook 4 to 5 more minutes.
**3.** Meanwhile, toast the hamburger buns and spread with ketchup, mustard and/or mayonnaise. Fill with the burgers and top with lettuce, tomato and/or red onion. Serve with pickles.

Per serving: Calories 523; Fat 30 g (Saturated 13 g); Cholesterol 116 mg; Sodium 426 mg; Carbohydrate 24 g; Fiber 2 g; Protein 37 g

## TOFU CUBAN SANDWICHES WITH JICAMA STICKS
ACTIVE: 40 min I TOTAL: 40 min I SERVES: 4

1   14-ounce package extra-firm tofu
1   small onion, sliced ¼ inch thick
3   cloves garlic, roughly chopped
1½  tablespoons extra-virgin olive oil
Juice of 2 oranges
1   medium jicama (about ¾ pound)
¼   teaspoon chili powder
4   small whole-wheat hoagie rolls, split
¼   cup yellow mustard
1¼  cups shredded low-fat low-sodium Swiss cheese (5 ounces)
⅔   cup chopped roasted red peppers, drained and rinsed
½   kosher dill pickle, chopped (about ¼ cup)

1. Lay the tofu on a cutting board and cut horizontally into 8 equal slices. Put in a shallow dish with the onion, garlic, olive oil and half of the orange juice and turn to coat; marinate 5 to 10 minutes.
2. Meanwhile, peel the jicama using a sharp knife and cut into sticks. Toss in a bowl with the remaining orange juice and the chili powder.
3. Heat a large nonstick skillet over medium-high heat. Turn the tofu to coat, add to the pan and cook until golden, 3 minutes per side. Transfer to a plate. Add the marinade to the pan and cook, stirring, 4 minutes.
4. Spread the cut sides of the rolls with the mustard and sprinkle with the cheese. Sandwich with the peppers, pickle, onion mixture and tofu.
5. Heat a large cast-iron skillet over medium heat. Working in batches, add the sandwiches and top with another heavy skillet to flatten; cook until golden brown and the cheese melts, 2 to 3 minutes per side. Serve with the jicama sticks.

Per serving: Calories 497; Fat 16 g (Saturated 4 g); Cholesterol 12 mg; Sodium 1,240 mg; Carbohydrate 59 g; Fiber 11 g; Protein 30 g

## RANCH CHICKEN SANDWICHES
ACTIVE: 25 min I TOTAL: 25 min I SERVES: 4

DONE IN
25
MINUTES

¼ cup plus 2 tablespoons buttermilk
2 to 3 dashes hot sauce
Kosher salt and freshly ground pepper
4 5-to-6-ounce chicken cutlets
1 small clove garlic
⅓ cup mayonnaise
2 teaspoons apple cider vinegar
2 tablespoons chopped fresh chives or scallions
4 slices pepper jack cheese
4 kaiser or onion rolls, split and toasted
Lettuce leaves and tomato slices, for topping
Potato chips, for serving (optional)

1. Preheat a grill or grill pan to medium high. Combine ¼ cup buttermilk, the hot sauce, ½ teaspoon salt, and pepper to taste in a large bowl. Add the chicken and turn to coat; let stand 10 minutes.
2. Meanwhile, make the ranch sauce: Mince the garlic with ¼ teaspoon salt on a cutting board; mash with the flat side of a chef's knife to make a paste. Combine the garlic paste, mayonnaise, vinegar, the remaining 2 tablespoons buttermilk and the chives in a small bowl. Season with salt and pepper.
3. Transfer the chicken to the grill, letting the excess marinade drip off. Grill until marked on the bottom, 3 to 4 minutes, then flip the chicken, top each piece with a slice of cheese and continue grilling until just cooked through, 2 to 4 more minutes.
4. Spread each roll with some of the ranch sauce and fill with the chicken, lettuce and tomato. Serve with potato chips.

Per serving: Calories 581; Fat 30 g (Saturated 8 g); Cholesterol 116 mg; Sodium 676 mg; Carbohydrate 34 g; Fiber 2 g; Protein 42 g

## BEEF PITA PIZZAS
ACTIVE: 30 min I TOTAL: 35 min I SERVES: 4

| | |
|---|---|
| 3 | tablespoons extra-virgin olive oil |
| 1 | medium onion, finely chopped |
| 1 | medium red bell pepper, finely chopped |
| 2 | tablespoons tomato paste |
| 8 | ounces 90% lean ground beef |

Kosher salt and freshly ground pepper

| | |
|---|---|
| ½ | cup plain 2% Greek yogurt |
| 1 | tablespoon plus 2 teaspoons red wine vinegar |
| 4 | whole-wheat pocketless pitas |
| 1 | head green-leaf lettuce, torn into pieces |
| ½ | cup pickled beets, cut into bite-size pieces |
| 1 | small cucumber, peeled and cut into half moons |

**1.** Position a rack in the upper third of the oven and preheat to 400°. Heat 1 tablespoon olive oil in a large nonstick skillet over medium-high heat. Add the onion and bell pepper and cook, stirring occasionally, until golden, 6 to 8 minutes. Add the tomato paste and cook, stirring, until brick red, 1 minute. Add the beef, 2 tablespoons water, ¾ teaspoon salt, and pepper to taste and cook, breaking up the meat, until browned, 3 to 4 minutes. Remove from the heat and stir in ¼ cup yogurt and 2 teaspoons vinegar. Season with salt and pepper and transfer to a bowl.

**2.** Wipe out the skillet and return to medium heat. Brush the pitas with 1 tablespoon olive oil, then lightly toast in the skillet, about 45 seconds per side. Arrange the pitas on a baking sheet and top evenly with the beef mixture. Transfer to the oven and bake 6 minutes.

**3.** Whisk the remaining ¼ cup yogurt, 1 tablespoon each olive oil and vinegar, and salt and pepper to taste in a bowl. Add the lettuce, beets and cucumber and toss. Slice the pizzas and serve with the salad.

Per serving: Calories 429; Fat 16 g (Saturated 3 g); Cholesterol 33 mg; Sodium 956 mg; Carbohydrate 52 g; Fiber 10 g; Protein 24 g

# Perfect
# Patties

## SLIDERS

Working on a piece of parchment paper, pat 1¼ pounds ground beef chuck into a 6-by-8-inch rectangle. Cut into twelve 2-inch squares; refrigerate at least 20 minutes. Season with ¾ teaspoon kosher salt, and pepper to taste. Heat a large cast-iron skillet over medium-high heat; add 1 tablespoon butter and let melt. Cook the patties until a crust forms, about 2 minutes per side, topping with cheese after flipping, if desired.

## STUFFED BURGERS

Gently shape 1½ pounds ground beef chuck into 4 balls. Press your thumb halfway into each to form a well. Pack 2 tablespoonfuls of shredded cheese into the middle of each ball. Shape the meat around the cheese and gently form into ¾-inch-thick patties. Chill at least 30 minutes. Preheat a grill to medium high and oil the grates. Season the patties with salt and pepper and grill 5 to 6 minutes per side.

## THIN BURGERS

Line an inverted baking sheet with parchment paper. Season 1 pound ground beef chuck with salt and pepper; form into 4 balls and set on the pan. Cover the meat with parchment and flatten with another baking sheet. Chill 1 hour. Heat a cast-iron skillet over medium-high heat and brush with oil. Cook the patties until a crust forms, 2 to 3 minutes per side; continue cooking until browned, 1 more minute per side, topping with cheese during the last minute, if desired.

## THICK BURGERS

Divide 2 pounds ground beef chuck into 4 pieces. Toss each piece back and forth between your hands to form a 1-inch-thick patty (do not overwork). Sprinkle generously all over with kosher salt; let sit 10 minutes at room temperature. Preheat a grill to medium high and oil the grates. Grill the burgers, covered, about 6 minutes per side, topping with cheese during the last 3 minutes, if desired. Let rest 2 minutes before serving.

# poultry

# TURKEY WITH WARM BARLEY SALAD
ACTIVE: 25 min **I** TOTAL: 30 min **I** SERVES: 4

2    cups fat-free low-sodium chicken broth
1    cup quick-cooking barley
Kosher salt
2    tablespoons unsalted butter
2    tablespoons sliced almonds
12   ounces Brussels sprouts, thinly sliced (about 3 cups)
Grated zest and juice of 1 lemon
1    tablespoon extra-virgin olive oil
4    4-to-5-ounce turkey cutlets (about ¼ inch thick)
Freshly ground pepper
1    plum tomato, diced

1. Bring the chicken broth and ¼ cup water to a boil in a medium saucepan. Stir in the barley and ¼ teaspoon salt, cover and cook over medium heat until the liquid is absorbed, about 10 minutes.
2. Meanwhile, melt 1 tablespoon butter in a large skillet over medium-high heat; add the almonds and cook, stirring, until toasted, 2 minutes. Transfer to a plate. Add the Brussels sprouts, lemon zest and ¼ teaspoon salt to the skillet and cook, stirring occasionally, until crisp-tender, about 2 minutes; transfer to a large bowl and wipe out the skillet. Add the barley to the bowl and toss; cover to keep warm.
3. Add the olive oil to the skillet and return to medium-high heat. Sprinkle the turkey with ¼ teaspoon salt, and pepper to taste; add to the skillet and cook, turning once, until cooked through, about 5 minutes. Divide among plates. Add the tomato and lemon juice to the skillet and cook 1 minute. Stir in the almonds and the remaining 1 tablespoon butter until melted, then spoon over the turkey. Serve with the barley salad.

Per serving: Calories 459; Fat 13 g (Saturated 4 g); Cholesterol 73 mg;
Sodium 551 mg; Carbohydrate 49 g; Fiber 12 g; Protein 40 g

LOW-
CALORIE
DINNER

# SLOW-COOKER TURKEY MOLE TACOS

ACTIVE: 15 min **I** TOTAL: 15 min (plus 8-hr slow cooking) **I** SERVES: 6

1   15-ounce can no-salt-added diced tomatoes, drained
2   large carrots, halved lengthwise and sliced crosswise
    into ½-inch-thick pieces
1   green bell pepper, diced
¼   cup roughly chopped fresh cilantro, plus more for topping
4   scallions, chopped, plus more for topping
2   tablespoons peanut butter (preferably natural)
1½  tablespoons low-sodium soy sauce
1   tablespoon ancho chile powder
2   teaspoons unsweetened cocoa powder
½   teaspoon Chinese five-spice powder or ground cinnamon
1   skinless, bone-in turkey breast (about 2½ pounds)
18  white corn tortillas

**1.** Combine the tomatoes, carrots, bell pepper, cilantro, scallions, peanut butter, soy sauce, chile powder, cocoa powder and Chinese five-spice powder in a 6-quart slow cooker and stir to combine. Add the turkey and turn to coat. Cover and cook on low, 8 hours.
**2.** Remove the turkey and transfer to a large plate; shred the meat off the bone with 2 forks. Return the shredded turkey to the slow cooker and stir to coat.
**3.** Warm the tortillas in a dry skillet or in the microwave. Serve the turkey in the tortillas and top with more cilantro and scallions.

Per serving: Calories 362; Fat 5 g (Saturated 1 g); Cholesterol 124 mg; Sodium 316 mg; Carbohydrate 26 g; Fiber 2 g; Protein 51 g

## TURKEY COBB SALAD

ACTIVE: 30 min  I  TOTAL: 30 min  I  SERVES: 4

LOW-
CALORIE
DINNER

| | |
|---|---|
| 4 | large eggs |
| 1⅛ | teaspoons smoked paprika |
| Kosher salt and freshly ground pepper | |
| 1½ | pounds turkey cutlets |
| 3 | tablespoons red wine vinegar |
| 3 | tablespoons extra-virgin olive oil |
| 1 | pint cherry tomatoes, halved |
| 2 | romaine lettuce hearts, chopped |
| ½ | avocado, peeled and chopped |
| ¼ | cup crumbled blue cheese (about 1 ounce) |

**1.** Put the eggs in a medium saucepan and cover with water by 2 inches; bring to a boil, then remove from the heat, cover and let stand 10 minutes. Transfer to a bowl of ice water to cool.

**2.** Meanwhile, preheat the broiler. Combine 1 teaspoon paprika, ¼ teaspoon salt, and pepper to taste in a small bowl. Arrange the turkey cutlets on a baking sheet and sprinkle both sides with the paprika mixture. Broil until just cooked through, about 3 minutes per side. Transfer to a plate and set aside while you make the dressing.

**3.** Combine the vinegar, the remaining ⅛ teaspoon paprika, ½ teaspoon salt, and pepper to taste in a large bowl. Whisk in the olive oil along with any collected juices from the turkey. Finely chop ¼ cup of the tomatoes and add to the dressing.

**4.** Peel and halve the hard-boiled eggs. Discard the yolks or save for another use. Chop the egg whites and add to the bowl with the dressing, along with the lettuce, avocado and the remaining 1¾ cups tomatoes. Chop the turkey, add to the bowl and toss. Divide the salad among bowls and sprinkle with the blue cheese.

Per serving: Calories 431; Fat 22 g (Saturated 5 g); Cholesterol 289 mg;
Sodium 700 mg; Carbohydrate 7 g; Fiber 3 g; Protein 51 g

# TURKEY AND QUINOA SALAD

ACTIVE: 35 min **I** TOTAL: 40 min **I** SERVES: 4

3      tablespoons extra-virgin olive oil
1½   cups quinoa, rinsed
Kosher salt
1      pound turkey cutlets
3      tablespoons chopped fresh tarragon and/or parsley
Freshly ground pepper
½     small red onion, halved and sliced
1½   pounds assorted heirloom tomatoes, chopped
1      Cubanelle chile pepper or other Italian frying pepper, seeded and chopped
4      Persian cucumbers, chopped
2      tablespoons sherry vinegar

**1.** Heat ½ tablespoon olive oil in a large skillet over medium-high heat. Add the quinoa and cook, stirring, until lightly toasted, about 4 minutes. Add 4 cups water and ¼ teaspoon salt and bring to a boil. Reduce the heat to medium and simmer until the water is absorbed and the quinoa is tender, about 15 minutes.
**2.** Toss the turkey with half of the herbs, ¼ teaspoon salt, and pepper to taste; set aside. Soak the onion slices in cold water, 10 minutes.
**3.** Toss the tomatoes, chile, cucumbers, vinegar, 1½ tablespoons olive oil, the remaining herbs, ¼ teaspoon salt, and pepper to taste in a large bowl. Drain the onion, add to the tomato mixture and toss.
**4.** Heat the remaining 1 tablespoon olive oil in a large nonstick skillet over medium-high heat. Working in batches, add the turkey and cook until golden, about 3 minutes per side. Drain on paper towels, then cut into 2-inch pieces. Fluff the quinoa with a fork and divide among bowls. Top with the tomato mixture and turkey.

Per serving: Calories 552; Fat 15 g (Saturated 2 g); Cholesterol 45 mg;
Sodium 483 mg; Carbohydrate 64 g; Fiber 9 g; Protein 41 g

## TURKEY TENDERS WITH CRANBERRY KETCHUP

ACTIVE: 30 min **I** TOTAL: 35 min **I** SERVES: 4

Kids' MEAL

| 1 | pound small carrots, greens trimmed |
| 4 | tablespoons unsalted butter, melted |
| Kosher salt and freshly ground pepper |
| 4 | cups cornflakes, finely crushed (about 1¾ cups crumbs) |
| Grated zest and juice of 1 lemon |
| 2 | tablespoons plus 1 teaspoon honey mustard |
| 1 | large egg white, lightly beaten |
| 1½ | pounds skinless, boneless turkey breast, cut into strips |
| 2 | cups cranberries (thawed, if frozen) |
| 1 | pear (such as Anjou or Bartlett), finely chopped |
| ½ | cup sugar |

**1.** Position racks in the upper and lower thirds of the oven and preheat to 450°. Place the carrots on a large sheet of foil; drizzle with 2 tablespoons melted butter and season with salt and pepper. Fold up the edges of the foil and add ¼ cup water, then seal into a packet. Set on a baking sheet and roast on the bottom oven rack until tender, 25 minutes.

**2.** Meanwhile, mix the cornflakes, the remaining 2 tablespoons melted butter, the lemon zest and ¼ teaspoon each salt and pepper in a shallow dish. Whisk 2 tablespoons mustard and the egg white in another dish. Coat the turkey in the mustard mixture; dredge in the cornflake mixture. Place on a wire rack set on a baking sheet. Roast on the top oven rack until cooked through, 15 minutes.

**3.** Combine the cranberries, pear, sugar, lemon juice and 2 tablespoons water in a small saucepan; bring to a boil, stirring. Reduce the heat to medium low; simmer until the cranberries burst, 5 minutes. Transfer to a blender, add the remaining 1 teaspoon mustard and puree until smooth. Season with salt and pepper. Serve with the turkey and carrots.

Per serving: Calories 547; Fat 13 g (Saturated 7 g); Cholesterol 98 mg; Sodium 778 mg; Carbohydrate 66 g; Fiber 7 g; Protein 47 g

## CHILI-RUBBED TURKEY CUTLETS WITH BLACK-EYED PEAS

ACTIVE: 30 min | TOTAL: 35 min | SERVES: 4

¾ teaspoon chili powder or Cajun seasoning
Juice of 1 lime
4 turkey cutlets (about 1¼ pounds)
1 cup Israeli couscous or other small pasta
3 tablespoons extra-virgin olive oil
1 ear of corn, kernels removed (or ¾ cup thawed frozen corn)
1 cup frozen black-eyed peas, thawed
1 stalk celery, finely chopped
¾ cup cherry tomatoes, halved
2 scallions, thinly sliced
2 tablespoons chopped fresh parsley or basil
Kosher salt and freshly ground pepper

1. Combine the chili powder and lime juice in a medium bowl. Add the turkey and turn to coat; let marinate 10 minutes.
2. Bring a medium saucepan of water to a boil. Add the couscous and cook until tender, 8 to 10 minutes; drain.
3. Meanwhile, heat 1 tablespoon olive oil in a large cast-iron skillet over medium-high heat. Add the corn, black-eyed peas and celery and cook, stirring occasionally, until they begin to soften, about 3 minutes. Add the tomatoes, scallions, parsley, ½ teaspoon salt, and pepper to taste and cook until warmed through, about 2 more minutes; transfer to a large bowl. Add the couscous to the bowl along with 1 tablespoon olive oil and salt and pepper to taste; toss.
4. Wipe out the skillet; add the remaining 1 tablespoon olive oil and heat over medium-high heat. Add the turkey and cook until browned, about 3 minutes per side; add salt and pepper. Serve with the couscous.

Per serving: Calories 470; Fat 12 g (Saturated 2 g); Cholesterol 56 mg; Sodium 396 mg; Carbohydrate 45 g; Fiber 6 g; Protein 44 g

## SLOPPY JOE BAKED POTATOES

ACTIVE: 30 min I TOTAL: 30 min I SERVES: 4

| | |
|---|---|
| 4 | russet potatoes |
| 2 | tablespoons unsalted butter |
| 1 | small onion, finely chopped |
| 1 | carrot, finely chopped |
| 1 | stalk celery, finely chopped |
| 1 | pound 93% lean ground turkey |

Kosher salt and freshly ground pepper

| | |
|---|---|
| ½ | cup ketchup |
| ⅓ | cup sweet chili sauce |
| 1 | tablespoon chili powder |
| ¼ | teaspoon garlic powder |
| ½ | cup shredded low-fat cheddar cheese (about 2 ounces) |

**1.** Pierce the potatoes in a few places with a fork; place on a microwave-safe plate and microwave until tender, turning once, about 15 minutes. Set aside.

**2.** Meanwhile, melt 1 tablespoon butter in a large skillet over medium heat. Add the onion, carrot and celery and cook, stirring occasionally, until the vegetables are tender, about 7 minutes. Add the turkey and ¼ teaspoon each salt and pepper; cook, breaking up the meat with a wooden spoon, until no longer pink on the surface, about 5 minutes. Stir in the ketchup, chili sauce, ½ cup water, the chili powder and garlic powder; continue cooking until the meat is cooked through, 3 to 5 more minutes.

**3.** Split open the baked potatoes lengthwise, dot with the remaining 1 tablespoon butter and gently fluff the flesh with a fork. Top with the turkey mixture and sprinkle with the cheese while still hot.

Per serving: Calories 494; Fat 15 g (Saturated 7 g); Cholesterol 87 mg; Sodium 1,295 mg; Carbohydrate 61 g; Fiber 4 g; Protein 32 g

Kids'
MEAL

# TURKEY MEATLOAF SQUARES
# WITH SWEET POTATOES

ACTIVE: 20 min **I** TOTAL: 35 min **I** SERVES: 4

4      medium sweet potatoes
Cooking spray
1      pound 93% lean ground turkey
1      small onion, grated
¾     cup panko breadcrumbs (preferably whole-wheat)
1      large egg, lightly beaten
⅓     cup ketchup
2      tablespoons hoisin sauce
1      1-inch piece ginger, peeled and grated
Kosher salt and freshly ground pepper
2      tablespoons unsalted butter, at room temperature
2      tablespoons chopped scallions or chives

**1.** Preheat the oven to 425°. Pierce the sweet potatoes all over with a fork
and microwave until tender, about 15 minutes.
**2.** Meanwhile, coat a rimmed baking sheet with cooking spray. Combine the
turkey, onion, panko and egg in a bowl. Add half each of the ketchup, hoisin
sauce and ginger and season with salt and pepper. Mix with your hands until
just combined. Form into a 9-by-11-inch rectangle on the prepared baking
sheet. Mix the remaining ketchup, hoisin sauce and ginger in a small bowl
with 2 tablespoons water; brush over the meat. Bake until golden and cooked
through, 12 to 15 minutes. Turn on the broiler and broil until the glaze is just
caramelized, 1 to 2 minutes.
**3.** Mix the butter, half of the scallions, ½ teaspoon salt, and pepper to taste
in a small bowl. Split the potatoes and top with the scallion butter. Slice the
meatloaf and serve with the potatoes. Sprinkle with the remaining scallions.

Per serving: Calories 414; Fat 14 g (Saturated 6 g); Cholesterol 134 mg;
Sodium 933 mg; Carbohydrate 46 g; Fiber 5 g; Protein 28 g

# STEWED CHICKEN AND CHICKPEAS

ACTIVE: 15 min **I** TOTAL: 35 min **I** SERVES: 4

1    14-ounce can no-salt-added tomato sauce
1    15-ounce can chickpeas, drained and rinsed
1    small bell pepper (any color), thinly sliced
⅓    cup dried apricots, halved
2    cloves garlic, smashed
¼    teaspoon garam masala or ground cinnamon, plus more for topping
Large pinch of red pepper flakes
Kosher salt
4    6-ounce skinless, boneless chicken breasts
¼    cup low-fat (2%) Greek yogurt
Chopped fresh parsley, for topping (optional)
3    whole-wheat pitas, quartered

**1.** Combine the tomato sauce, 1 cup water, the chickpeas, bell pepper, apricots, garlic, garam masala, red pepper flakes and ½ teaspoon salt in a large skillet and bring to a simmer over medium-high heat. Nestle the chicken in the tomato-chickpea mixture; reduce the heat to maintain a gentle simmer and cook, uncovered, turning the chicken once, until cooked through, about 20 minutes.

**2.** Divide the chicken and tomato-chickpea mixture among plates, top with the yogurt and sprinkle with parsley and garam masala to taste. Serve with the pita wedges.

Per serving: Calories 461; Fat 4 g (Saturated 1 g); Cholesterol 100 mg; Sodium 369 mg; Carbohydrate 55 g; Fiber 10 g; Protein 52 g

# CHICKEN CACCIATORE
ACTIVE: 30 min I TOTAL: 40 min I SERVES: 4

8    small skin-on, bone-in chicken thighs, trimmed of excess fat (2 to 2½ pounds)
Kosher salt
¼    cup all-purpose flour
2    tablespoons extra-virgin olive oil
1    large onion, cut into wedges
2    sprigs rosemary
½ to ¾ teaspoon red pepper flakes
½    cup dry white wine
1    28-ounce can whole San Marzano tomatoes, crushed by hand
1    cup instant polenta
Freshly ground pepper

1. Rinse the chicken and pat dry; sprinkle with 1 teaspoon salt, then toss with the flour. Heat the olive oil in a Dutch oven or deep skillet over medium-high heat. Add the chicken, skin-side down; cover and cook until browned, 5 to 6 minutes per side. Transfer to a plate and set aside.

2. Add the onion, rosemary and red pepper flakes to the pot and cook, stirring occasionally, until the onion starts to brown, about 4 minutes. Add the wine, scraping up any browned bits from the bottom of the pot. Stir in the tomatoes and ½ cup water.

3. Return the chicken to the pot, skin-side up. Cover and bring to a rapid simmer. Uncover, spoon the sauce over the chicken and continue simmering until cooked through, about 8 more minutes.

4. Meanwhile, cook the polenta as the label directs; season with salt and pepper. Serve with the chicken.

Per serving: Calories 695; Fat 36 g (Saturated 9 g); Cholesterol 158 mg; Sodium 658 mg; Carbohydrate 45 g; Fiber 6 g; Protein 38 g

# CHICKEN AND CHORIZO RICE

ACTIVE: 30 min **I** TOTAL: 40 min **I** SERVES: 4

¼ cup extra-virgin olive oil
1 medium onion, chopped
2 cloves garlic, minced
4 skinless, boneless chicken thighs (about 1½ pounds)
Kosher salt and freshly ground pepper
1½ cups sliced dried chorizo (about 7 ounces)
3 tablespoons tomato paste
2 cups converted rice
3 tablespoons capers packed in brine
3½ cups fat-free low-sodium chicken broth
1 cup frozen peas
Lemon wedges, for serving

**1.** Heat the olive oil in a large heavy skillet or pot over high heat. Add the onion and garlic and cook, stirring, until the onion is translucent, about 3 minutes.
**2.** Season the chicken with ¼ teaspoon each salt and pepper. Add to the skillet along with the chorizo; cook, turning occasionally, until the chicken starts to brown, about 3 minutes. Move the chicken and chorizo to one side of the pan and stir in the tomato paste, rice and capers. Add the broth and bring to a boil. Cook, stirring occasionally, about 8 minutes. Stir in the peas, reduce the heat to medium low, cover and cook until the rice is tender, about 15 minutes. Let rest, covered, 5 minutes.
**3.** Fluff the rice with a fork, stirring to combine all the ingredients. Serve with lemon wedges.

Per serving: Calories 985; Fat 41 g (Saturated 11 g); Cholesterol 207 mg;
Sodium 1,311 mg; Carbohydrate 89 g; Fiber 4 g; Protein 61 g

## CHICKEN FAJITAS

ACTIVE: 35 min  I  TOTAL: 35 min  I  SERVES: 4

1  teaspoon chili powder
¾  teaspoon ground cumin
Kosher salt and freshly ground pepper
1  pound skinless, boneless chicken breasts
2  tablespoons extra-virgin olive oil
2  bell peppers (any color), sliced
1  red onion, sliced
2  cloves garlic, finely chopped
½  teaspoon grated lime zest, plus wedges for serving
8  corn tortillas
½  cup prepared pico de gallo or fresh salsa
⅓  cup crumbled cotija cheese (about 1½ ounces)

**1.** Preheat the oven to 425°. Mix the chili powder, ½ teaspoon cumin, and ¼ teaspoon each salt and pepper and rub on the chicken breasts.
**2.** Heat 1 tablespoon olive oil in a large skillet over medium-high heat. Add the chicken and cook, turning, until golden, 4 to 5 minutes. Transfer to a baking sheet, reserving the skillet, and bake until just cooked through, 8 to 10 minutes. Transfer to a cutting board to rest, 5 minutes.
**3.** Meanwhile, heat the remaining 1 tablespoon olive oil in the reserved skillet over medium heat. Add the bell peppers, onion, garlic and the remaining ¼ teaspoon cumin and cook, stirring, until the vegetables are lightly browned, 8 minutes. Stir in the lime zest and 2 tablespoons water. Season with salt.
**4.** Wrap the tortillas in foil and warm in the oven, 5 minutes, then divide among plates. Slice the chicken. Top the tortillas with the chicken, bell pepper mixture, pico de gallo and cheese. Serve with lime wedges.

Per serving: Calories 372; Fat 13 g (Saturated 3 g); Cholesterol 75 mg;
Sodium 779 mg; Carbohydrate 33 g; Fiber 4 g; Protein 32 g

## CHICKEN AND RICE CASSEROLE

ACTIVE: 20 min I TOTAL: 40 min I SERVES: 4

| | |
|---|---|
| 2 | tablespoons unsalted butter |
| 2 | cloves garlic, finely chopped |
| 4 | scallions, sliced |
| 2 | cups broccoli florets |
| 2 | cups shredded rotisserie chicken, skin removed |
| 1 | cup medium-grain white rice |
| 1 | plum tomato, chopped |

Kosher salt and freshly ground pepper

| | |
|---|---|
| 2 | cups low-sodium chicken broth |
| ¼ | cup sour cream |
| 1 | cup diced dill havarti cheese (about 4 ounces) |
| ¼ | cup grated parmesan cheese (about 1 ounce) |

**1.** Preheat the oven to 425°. Melt the butter in a large ovenproof skillet over medium heat. Add the garlic and about three-quarters of the scallions and cook, stirring occasionally, until soft, about 2 minutes. Add the broccoli, chicken, rice, tomato, 1 teaspoon salt, and pepper to taste; stir to combine.

**2.** Whisk the chicken broth and sour cream in a bowl, pour into the skillet and bring to a simmer. Stir in half each of the havarti and parmesan. Cover tightly with a lid or foil, transfer to the oven and bake until the rice is tender and most of the liquid is absorbed, about 20 minutes.

**3.** Turn on the broiler. Uncover the skillet and sprinkle with the remaining havarti and parmesan, then broil until golden, about 2 minutes. Sprinkle with the reserved scallions.

Per serving: Calories 626; Fat 32 g (Saturated 16 g); Cholesterol 186 mg;
Sodium 1,299 mg; Carbohydrate 38 g; Fiber 3 g; Protein 45 g

# CHICKEN-ZUCCHINI CHILAQUILES
ACTIVE: 20 min I TOTAL: 30 min I SERVES: 4

½    cup vegetable oil
15   corn tortillas, quartered
1    small zucchini, cut into ½-inch pieces
2    cups shredded rotisserie chicken, skin removed
1    cup tomatillo salsa
½    cup chopped fresh cilantro, plus more for topping
1    cup shredded mozzarella or Mexican cheese blend
Sliced radishes and chopped red onion, for topping

1. Heat the vegetable oil in a large skillet over medium-high heat. Add half of the tortillas and cook, turning with tongs, until golden, about 3 minutes; drain on paper towels. Repeat with the remaining tortillas.

2. Reduce the heat to medium and add the zucchini; cook, stirring occasionally, until crisp-tender, about 2 minutes. Stir in the chicken, tomatillo salsa, ¾ cup water and the cilantro; bring to a simmer and cook 2 minutes.

3. Meanwhile, preheat the broiler. Spread half of the fried tortillas in an 8-inch-square baking dish. Top with about half of the chicken mixture and ½ cup cheese. Cover with the remaining tortillas, then the remaining chicken mixture and cheese. Broil until the cheese is melted, 2 to 3 minutes. Serve topped with radishes, red onion and cilantro.

Per serving: Calories 821; Fat 49 g (Saturated 10 g); Cholesterol 128 mg; Sodium 975 mg; Carbohydrate 59 g; Fiber 4 g; Protein 39 g

# CHIPOTLE CHICKEN BURRITOS

ACTIVE: 30 min I TOTAL: 30 min I SERVES: 4

| | |
|---|---|
| 1 | tablespoon vegetable oil |
| ¾ | cup pico de gallo or fresh salsa |
| 1 | chipotle chile in adobo sauce, chopped, plus 1 to 2 tablespoons sauce from the can |
| 1 | 14-ounce can pinto beans, drained and rinsed |
| 1½ | cups shredded rotisserie chicken, skin removed |
| ¼ | cup roughly chopped fresh cilantro |

Kosher salt

| | |
|---|---|
| 4 | burrito-size flour tortillas |
| 1⅓ | cups cooked white rice, warmed |
| 1⅓ | cups shredded monterey jack cheese (about 5 ounces) |
| 1⅓ | cups shredded romaine lettuce |

Guacamole, for serving (optional)

**1.** Heat the vegetable oil in a medium pot over medium-high heat. Add ½ cup pico de gallo, the chopped chipotle, and adobo sauce to taste; cook until the mixture starts to sizzle, about 2 minutes. Add the beans and ¾ cup water; bring to a low boil, then stir in the chicken and cook until the mixture is slightly thickened, about 2 minutes. Stir in the cilantro and season with salt.

**2.** Heat the tortillas as the label directs. Arrange the rice horizontally in the lower half of each tortilla, leaving a 1½-inch border on all sides. Top evenly with the cheese, chicken mixture, lettuce and the remaining pico de gallo.

**3.** Fold the bottom edge of each tortilla snugly over the filling, tuck in the sides and roll up tightly. Cut the burritos in half and serve with guacamole.

Per serving: Calories 731; Fat 30 g (Saturated 11 g); Cholesterol 117 mg;
Sodium 1,501 mg; Carbohydrate 70 g; Fiber 8 g; Protein 43 g

## GRILLED CHICKEN WITH BULGUR

ACTIVE: 15 min I TOTAL: 35 min I SERVES: 4

| | |
|---|---|
| 4 | chicken legs (drumsticks and thighs attached; about 2½ pounds) |
| 2 | tablespoons extra-virgin olive oil |
| ¼ | teaspoon ground cinnamon |
| ¼ | teaspoon ground ginger |
| ¼ | teaspoon cayenne pepper |

Kosher salt

| | |
|---|---|
| 2 | cups green or red grapes (in clusters) |
| 1 | tablespoon unsalted butter |
| ½ | teaspoon grated lemon zest |
| 1 | cup bulgur |
| 2 | scallions, sliced |
| ¼ | cup chopped fresh parsley |

1. Preheat a grill to medium high. Coat the chicken legs with 1 tablespoon olive oil, then sprinkle all over with the cinnamon, ginger, cayenne and ¾ teaspoon salt. Transfer to the grill, skin-side up; cover and cook 12 minutes. Flip the chicken, cover and continue cooking until the skin is golden brown and a thermometer inserted into the thickest part registers 160°, 10 to 15 more minutes. Grill the grapes, covered but turning occasionally, until slightly charred, about 6 minutes.
2. Meanwhile, combine 1½ cups water, the butter, lemon zest and a pinch of salt in a medium saucepan; bring to a boil. Add the bulgur, reduce the heat to medium low and simmer, covered, until tender, about 15 minutes. (Drain any excess water, if necessary.)
3. Fluff the bulgur with a fork and stir in the grilled grapes, discarding the stems. Stir in the scallions, parsley and the remaining 1 tablespoon olive oil; season with salt. Serve with the chicken.

Per serving: Calories 444; Fat 19 g (Saturated 6 g); Cholesterol 112 mg; Sodium 588 mg; Carbohydrate 35 g; Fiber 7 g; Protein 34 g

## SESAME-LEMON CHICKEN

ACTIVE: 30 min I TOTAL: 35 min I SERVES: 4

| | |
|---|---|
| 1 | tablespoon toasted sesame seeds |
| 1 | tablespoon finely grated lemon zest |
| 2 | teaspoons dried thyme |
| ½ | teaspoon sugar |

Kosher salt and freshly ground pepper

| | |
|---|---|
| 8 | skin-on, bone-in chicken thighs, trimmed (2 to 2½ pounds) |
| 1 | tablespoon fresh lemon juice |
| 2 | tablespoons red wine vinegar |
| 2 | tablespoons extra-virgin olive oil |
| 2 | romaine lettuce hearts, chopped (about 8 cups) |
| 1 | cucumber, chopped |
| 1 | tomato, chopped |
| 2 | cups lightly salted pita chips, crushed |

1. Preheat the broiler. Make the rub: Combine the sesame seeds, lemon zest, thyme, sugar, ½ teaspoon salt and ¼ teaspoon pepper in a spice grinder; pulse until the seeds are slightly cracked.
2. Season the chicken with salt and all but about 1½ tablespoons of the rub. Set skin-side down on a broiler pan and broil, flipping the chicken and rotating the pan halfway through, until the chicken is golden and a meat thermometer registers 170°, 8 to 10 minutes per side.
3. Make the dressing: Mix 1 tablespoon of the reserved rub, the lemon juice, vinegar, and salt to taste in a bowl. Whisk in the olive oil.
4. When the chicken is done, whisk 1 tablespoon of the pan drippings into the dressing. Add the lettuce, cucumber, tomato and pita chips; season with salt and pepper and toss. Sprinkle the chicken with the remaining ½ tablespoon rub and serve with the salad.

Per serving: Calories 356; Fat 17 g (Saturated 3 g); Cholesterol 107 mg;
Sodium 777 mg; Carbohydrate 22 g; Fiber 5 g; Protein 30 g

## ROAST CHICKEN WITH APPLE SLAW
ACTIVE: 20 min I TOTAL: 40 min I SERVES: 4

| | |
|---|---|
| 2 | half chickens (about 4 pounds total) |

Kosher salt
Juice of 2 limes, plus wedges for serving

| | |
|---|---|
| ¼ | teaspoon ground allspice |
| 3 | tablespoons Sriracha (Asian chile sauce) |
| 3 | tablespoons honey |
| ⅓ | cup mayonnaise |
| 1 | Granny Smith apple |
| 4 | cups shredded coleslaw mix |
| 3 | scallions, sliced |

1. Preheat the oven to 450° and line a rimmed baking sheet with foil. Pat the chicken dry and sprinkle with 1 teaspoon salt. Place skin-side up on the prepared baking sheet and roast until the skin begins to turn golden, about 25 minutes.

2. Meanwhile, make the glaze: Mix the juice of 1 lime with the allspice and 2 tablespoons each Sriracha and honey in a small bowl; set aside. Make the slaw: Whisk the juice of the remaining lime, 1 tablespoon each Sriracha and honey, and the mayonnaise in a medium bowl. Cut the apple into matchsticks and add to the mayonnaise mixture along with the coleslaw mix and scallions; toss to coat. Season with salt.

3. Remove the chicken from the oven and brush with the glaze; return to the oven and continue roasting until the skin is golden brown and crisp and a thermometer inserted into the thickest part of the chicken registers 165°, 7 to 10 more minutes. Transfer the chicken to a cutting board and cut each piece in half. Serve with the apple slaw and lime wedges.

Per serving: Calories 457; Fat 26 g (Saturated 5 g); Cholesterol 100 mg; Sodium 979 mg; Carbohydrate 25 g; Fiber 4 g; Protein 31 g

## KALE-SESAME CHICKEN SALAD

ACTIVE: 25 min **I** TOTAL: 35 min **I** SERVES: 4

LOW-CALORIE DINNER

| | |
|---|---|
| 3 | tablespoons low-sodium soy sauce |
| 2 | tablespoons maple syrup (preferably grade B) |
| ¼ | teaspoon red pepper flakes |
| ¼ | cup plus 2 tablespoons fresh lemon juice (from 2 to 3 lemons) |
| 1 | pound skinless, boneless chicken breasts |
| 1½ | pounds sweet potatoes (about 2 large) |
| 2 | firm apples (such as Cortland or Pink Lady) |
| 1 | English cucumber |
| 1 | 5-ounce package baby kale (about 8 cups) |
| 1 | tablespoon sesame seeds |
| 1 | tablespoon toasted sesame oil |

Kosher salt and freshly ground pepper

1 tablespoon chopped salted peanuts

**1.** Bring the soy sauce, maple syrup, red pepper flakes, ¼ cup lemon juice and 1 cup water to a boil in a wide saucepan. Add the chicken in a single layer; reduce the heat to medium low. Cover and simmer, turning occasionally, until just cooked through, 10 to 15 minutes. Remove the chicken to a plate (reserve the liquid). Let cool, then shred.

**2.** Peel the sweet potatoes and cut into ½-inch cubes. Add to the liquid in the saucepan; cook over medium heat, stirring occasionally, until just tender, about 15 minutes. Transfer to a plate with a slotted spoon (reserve the liquid). Let the potatoes and liquid cool.

**3.** Cut the apples into matchsticks. Peel the cucumber, cut in half lengthwise and thinly slice. Combine the apples, cucumber, kale, sesame seeds, chicken, sweet potatoes and sesame oil in a large bowl. Toss with the reserved cooking liquid and the remaining 2 tablespoons lemon juice. Season with salt and pepper; sprinkle with the peanuts.

Per serving: Calories 434; Fat 8 g (Saturated 1 g); Cholesterol 66 mg; Sodium 604 mg; Carbohydrate 60 g; Fiber 9 g; Protein 33 g

# CHICKEN-BROCCOLI STIR-FRY

ACTIVE: 20 min I TOTAL: 30 min I SERVES: 4

LOW-
CALORIE
DINNER

Kosher salt
1    bunch broccoli (about 1 pound), cut into florets
1    8-ounce package rice noodles
¼    cup sugar
1    tablespoon vegetable oil
5    cloves garlic, thinly sliced
1    pound skinless, boneless chicken thighs, cut into ½-inch chunks
1 to 2 tablespoons fish sauce
1    red chile pepper (such as Fresno), seeded and sliced (optional)
¼    cup fresh cilantro leaves, chopped, plus more for topping
Freshly ground pepper
2    scallions, thinly sliced, plus more for topping

1. Bring a large saucepan of salted water to a boil. Add the broccoli and cook, stirring, until bright green and crisp-tender, about 3 minutes. Use a slotted spoon to transfer to a large bowl. Add the rice noodles to the water and return to a boil. Remove from the heat and let soak while you prepare the chicken, stirring occasionally.
2. Combine the sugar and 1 tablespoon water in a large skillet over medium-high heat, stirring until the sugar dissolves. Cook, undisturbed, until the mixture is dark amber, about 3 minutes. Carefully stir in the vegetable oil and garlic and cook until the garlic is golden, about 30 seconds. Add the chicken and fish sauce and cook, stirring, until the chicken is no longer pink, about 2 minutes. Remove from the heat and stir in the chile pepper, cilantro and ¼ teaspoon pepper.
3. Drain the noodles and add to the bowl with the broccoli. Add the scallions and chicken and toss. Divide among plates and top with more cilantro and scallions.

Per serving: Calories 435; Fat 6 g (Saturated 2 g); Cholesterol 94 mg;
Sodium 573 mg; Carbohydrate 63 g; Fiber 3 g; Protein 27 g

# SKILLET CHICKEN AND ARTICHOKES

ACTIVE: 25 min **I** TOTAL: 30 min **I** SERVES: 4

LOW-
CALORIE
DINNER

4    6-to-8-ounce skinless, boneless chicken breasts
Kosher salt and freshly ground pepper
3    tablespoons extra-virgin olive oil
1    9-ounce package frozen artichoke hearts, thawed and patted dry
1    small red onion, cut into wedges
3    cloves garlic, thinly sliced
1    teaspoon dried oregano
¾    cup low-sodium chicken broth
¼    cup pitted kalamata olives
¼    cup chopped fresh parsley
¼    cup crumbled feta cheese
¼    cup sliced Peppadew peppers, plus 2 teaspoons brine from the jar

**1.** Place the chicken breasts between 2 pieces of plastic wrap and pound with a skillet until about ½ inch thick. Season with salt and pepper. Heat 1 tablespoon olive oil in a large nonstick skillet over medium-high heat. Add the chicken and cook, undisturbed, until golden on the bottom, 4 to 5 minutes; turn and cook until the other side is golden, 2 to 3 more minutes. Transfer to a plate and set aside.
**2.** Wipe out the skillet and return to medium-high heat. Add the remaining 2 tablespoons olive oil; when hot, add the artichoke hearts and red onion and cook, undisturbed, until golden in spots, about 1 minute. Season with salt and pepper and continue cooking, stirring occasionally, until the vegetables are tender, about 2 more minutes. Add the garlic and oregano and cook, stirring, 30 seconds.
**3.** Return the chicken to the skillet and add the broth and olives. Bring to a gentle simmer, cover and cook until the chicken is cooked through, 4 to 6 minutes. Top with the parsley, feta, Peppadews and brine.

Per serving: Calories 364; Fat 16 g (Saturated 4 g); Cholesterol 112 mg; Sodium 586 mg; Carbohydrate 10 g; Fiber 5 g; Protein 44 g

## CHICKEN AND APPLE SALAD
ACTIVE: 30 min **I** TOTAL: 40 min **I** SERVES: 4

2     skin-on, bone-in chicken breasts (about 2 pounds)
Kosher salt and freshly ground pepper
⅓     cup plus 1 tablespoon vegetable oil
2     tablespoons sherry vinegar or red wine vinegar
1     tablespoon plus 1 teaspoon dijon mustard
1     teaspoon honey
2     Gala apples
½     cup chopped walnuts
1     small head escarole, torn into pieces
2     heads Belgian endive, trimmed, halved lengthwise
      and thinly sliced
4     ounces aged cheddar cheese, shredded (about 1 cup)
Multigrain bread, for serving (optional)

1. Preheat the oven to 375˚. Season the chicken with 1 teaspoon salt, and pepper to taste. Heat 1 tablespoon vegetable oil in a large ovenproof skillet over medium-high heat. Add the chicken, skin-side down, and cook until golden, about 5 minutes. Transfer the skillet to the oven (do not flip the chicken); roast until a thermometer inserted into the thickest part of the meat registers 165˚, about 25 minutes. Transfer to a cutting board and let rest 5 minutes.
2. Meanwhile, make the dressing: Whisk the vinegar, mustard and honey in a large bowl. Gradually add the remaining ⅓ cup vegetable oil, whisking until emulsified.
3. Remove the chicken from the bone; slice. Thinly slice the apples and add to the dressing along with the walnuts, escarole and endive; season with salt and pepper. Toss the salad and top with the chicken and cheese. Serve with bread.

Per serving: Calories 754; Fat 53 g (Saturated 12 g); Cholesterol 149 mg; Sodium 910 mg; Carbohydrate 19 g; Fiber 8 g; Protein 54 g

# Chicken Breasts
# 50 Ways

No. **46**

**1. Basic Sautéed** Season 4 small chicken breasts with salt and pepper. Cook in 2 tablespoons vegetable oil in a large skillet over medium heat until golden, turning once, 12 minutes. Cover; cook 3 more minutes.

**2. Lemon-Thyme** Cook Basic Sautéed Chicken (No. 1) in 1 tablespoon each butter and oil. When done, stir in 1 tablespoon each butter and lemon juice, 4 strips lemon zest and 2 thyme sprigs; turn the chicken to coat.

**3. Blue Cheese–Shallot** Make Basic Sautéed Chicken (No. 1); remove to a plate. Cook 3 sliced shallots in the drippings, 2 minutes. Add ¾ cup chicken broth; simmer 5 minutes. Stir in 1 tablespoon butter. Pour over the chicken; top with blue cheese.

**4. Hoisin-Plum** Make Basic Sautéed Chicken (No. 1); remove to a plate. Cook 4 diced plums and 1 bunch chopped scallions in the drippings, 2 minutes. Add ½ cup chicken broth and ¼ cup hoisin sauce; simmer 5 minutes. Stir in the juice of 1 lime; pour over the chicken.

**5. Apple-Mustard** Make Basic Sautéed Chicken (No. 1); remove to a plate. Cook 1 chopped apple in the drippings, 2 minutes. Add ⅔ cup chicken broth; simmer until reduced by half. Stir in 1 tablespoon grainy mustard; pour over the chicken.

**6. Stuffed** Mix ¾ cup shredded mozzarella, 2 ounces goat cheese and 1 tablespoon chopped chives. Cut a pocket in the side of 4 small chicken breasts; fill with the cheese. Cook as for Basic Sautéed Chicken (No. 1).

**7. Saltimbocca** Make Basic Sautéed Chicken (No. 1), topping each breast with 2 sage leaves and wrapping with 2 slices of prosciutto before cooking. Top each with a slice of provolone during the last minute.

**8. Mushroom** Make Basic Sautéed Chicken (No. 1); remove to a plate. Cook 1 chopped shallot and 1 pound sliced mushrooms in the drippings, 4 minutes. Add ¾ cup red wine and 1 cup chicken broth; cook until reduced by half. Stir in 2 tablespoons each butter and chopped parsley; pour over the chicken.

**9. Piccata** Make Basic Sautéed Chicken (No. 1); remove to a plate. Add the juice of 2 lemons and ¾ cup chicken broth to the drippings; simmer until reduced by half. Stir in 2 tablespoons each capers, chopped parsley and butter; pour over the chicken.

**10. Leek-Grape** Make Basic Sautéed Chicken (No. 1), adding 1 chopped leek before covering. Remove the chicken to a plate. Add 2 cups grapes and ½ cup each cream and chicken broth to the pan; simmer until reduced by half. Add 1 tablespoon grainy mustard and some chopped parsley; pour over the chicken.

**11. Alla Vodka** Make Basic Sautéed Chicken (No. 1); remove to a plate. Add 3 sliced garlic cloves and 1 tablespoon butter to the drippings; cook 1 minute. Add 2 cups canned crushed tomatoes, ½ cup cream and ¼ cup vodka; simmer 5 minutes. Pour over the chicken and top with chopped basil.

**12. Breaded** Pound 4 small chicken breasts until ½ inch thick; season with salt. Dredge in flour, dip in 2 beaten eggs, then dredge in breadcrumbs. Cook in 3 tablespoons olive oil over medium heat until golden, 3 minutes per side; drain on paper towels. Season with salt.

**13. Cornflake** Make Breaded Chicken (No. 12), swapping 2 cups crushed cornflakes mixed with 1 teaspoon paprika for the breadcrumbs. Cook only 2 minutes per side.

**14. Parmesan** Make Breaded Chicken (No. 12), mixing the breadcrumbs with equal parts grated parmesan. Arrange the cooked chicken in a baking dish; top with 2 cups marinara sauce, 1 cup grated mozzarella and ½ cup parmesan. Bake at 425°, 15 minutes.

**15. Gravy-Topped** Make Breaded Chicken (No. 12); remove to a plate. Whisk 1 tablespoon flour, a pinch of paprika, and pepper to taste into the drippings; cook, whisking, until golden. Whisk in 1 cup milk; simmer until thick. Pour over the chicken.

**16. Spice-Crusted** Make Breaded Chicken (No. 12), substituting 1 cup fine cornmeal mixed with 1½ teaspoons ground cumin and ¼ teaspoon cayenne for the breadcrumbs.

**17. Nuggets** Cut 2 large chicken breasts into 1-inch pieces; season with salt. Dip in buttermilk, then dredge in 1 cup flour mixed with 2 teaspoons Cajun seasoning. Fry in 2 inches of 365° vegetable oil, 4 minutes.

**18. Spicy Tenders** Cut 4 small chicken breasts into strips. Dredge in flour, then dip in 4 beaten eggs mixed with 1 tablespoon each Sriracha and water; dredge in panko. Fry in 1 inch of 350° vegetable oil, 6 minutes. Serve with mayonnaise mixed with Sriracha.

**19. Pesto Pasta** Brown 1 sliced large chicken breast in a skillet with olive oil over medium-high heat, turning, 5 minutes. Add ½ cup white wine; simmer until reduced, 5 minutes. Add ⅓ cup pesto and ¾ cup cream; cook until thickened. Stir in ¼ cup parmesan; season with salt and pepper. Toss with 12 ounces cooked pasta.

**20. Basic Soup** Simmer 5 cups chicken broth, 2 large chicken breasts and 1 cup each sliced carrots, celery, onions and parsnips, 20 minutes. Shred the chicken, then return to the soup; add some chopped dill and parsley.

**21. Dumpling Soup** Make Basic Chicken Soup (No. 20). Mix ⅓ cup each flour and softened butter to form a paste; whisk into the soup. Bring to a boil. Add 4 quartered rounds of refrigerated biscuit dough; cover and simmer 25 minutes.

**22. Basic Roasted** Season 2 large chicken breasts with salt and pepper. Brown in an ovenproof skillet in 1 tablespoon olive oil over medium heat, turning once, 8 minutes, then roast at 375°, 15 minutes.

**23. Ratatouille** Prepare Basic Roasted Chicken (No. 22); remove to a plate after browning. Sauté 1 each diced small eggplant, zucchini, bell pepper, tomato and red onion in the drippings, 5 minutes. Stir in a pinch of sugar and 1 tablespoon red wine vinegar. Return the chicken to the pan; roast at 375°, 15 minutes. Top with torn basil.

**24. Potato-Leek** Prepare Basic Roasted Chicken (No. 22); remove to a plate after browning. Sauté 3 chopped leeks and 1½ pounds diced potatoes in the drippings, 7 minutes. Return the chicken to the pan; roast at 375°, 15 minutes. Stir in 1 tablespoon each butter, chopped dill and parsley.

**25. Maple-Squash** Toss 3 cups diced butternut squash, 1 cup pecans and 2 tablespoons each maple syrup and diced butter on a foil-lined baking sheet. Make Basic Roasted Chicken (No. 22) on the baking sheet with the squash.

**26. Pizza** Make Basic Roasted Chicken (No. 22) with 1 chicken breast; shred. Toss with 1 pint halved cherry tomatoes, 2 sliced bell peppers, 1 sliced onion, ¼ cup olive oil and 1 tablespoon Italian seasoning; spread on 1 pound rolled-out pizza dough. Bake on a hot stone at 475°, 15 to 20 minutes.

**27. New Orleans–Style** Make Basic Roasted Chicken (No. 22), rubbing the meat with 1 tablespoon each Cajun seasoning and brown sugar before browning. Mix ½ cup each chopped giardiniera and olives with ¼ cup each olive oil and chopped parsley; serve with the chicken.

**28. Kebabs** Cut 2 each small chicken breasts, Italian sausages, bell peppers and red onions into 1-inch pieces. Marinate in ¼ cup olive oil, the juice of 1 lemon, 3 smashed garlic cloves and a pinch each of salt and Italian seasoning in the refrigerator, 30 minutes. Thread onto skewers; grill over medium-high heat, 4 to 5 minutes per side.

**29. Pho** Simmer 4 cups chicken broth, 2 tablespoons fish sauce, 1 star anise pod and 1 cinnamon stick, 10 minutes. Add 2 large sliced chicken breasts and cook 10 minutes. Add 8 ounces cooked rice noodles. Top with sliced jalapeño, basil and mint.

**30. Peanut Stir-Fry** Mix 3 tablespoons each soy sauce, chili-garlic sauce and water with 1 tablespoon cornstarch. Heat 2 tablespoons vegetable oil in a skillet over high heat; add 4 cubed small chicken breasts, 1 tablespoon minced ginger and ½ cup each peanuts and sliced celery. Stir-fry 5 minutes. Add the sauce; cook until thick.

No. **31**

No. **45**

No. **38**

No. **14**

No. 42

**31. Fried Rice** Scramble 3 eggs in a skillet in 2 tablespoons vegetable oil over high heat; remove to a bowl. Heat 1 more tablespoon oil in the skillet. Add ½ chopped onion, 1½ cups chopped broccoli and 1 teaspoon each sugar and kosher salt; cook, stirring, 3 minutes. Add 2 cubed small chicken breasts; stir-fry 5 minutes. Add 3 cups cooked rice and the eggs; stir until hot.

**32. Tomato Fried Rice** Make Fried Rice (No. 31), swapping ¾ cup diced tomato and 1 bunch chopped scallions for the broccoli.

**33. Oven-Fried** Mix ½ cup mayonnaise and ¼ cup dijon mustard. Add 4 small chicken breasts; turn to coat. Dredge in 2 cups crushed cornflakes mixed with 1 teaspoon paprika; bake at 400°, 15 to 20 minutes.

**34. Basic Poached** Cover 2 large chicken breasts with cold water in a pot; add 1 tablespoon kosher salt. Bring to a gentle simmer; cook until just firm, 15 minutes. Plunge into salted ice water, 30 seconds, then drain.

**35. Creamy Salad** Make Basic Poached Chicken (No. 34); dice. Mix with ½ cup mayonnaise, ¼ cup each sour cream and chopped parsley, 2 chopped celery stalks and 2 tablespoons chopped celery leaves.

**36. French Salad** Make Basic Poached Chicken (No. 34); dice. Mix with ⅔ cup mayonnaise, 2 teaspoons dijon mustard and ¼ cup chopped mixed herbs.

**37. Chopped Salad** Make Basic Poached Chicken (No. 34); chop. Toss with chopped tomatoes, avocado, cucumber, cilantro, and salt and pepper. Top with minced red onion, olive oil and lime juice.

**38. Barbecue Sandwiches** Make Basic Poached Chicken (No. 34); shred. Warm ¼ cup cider vinegar, 2 tablespoons brown sugar, 1 tablespoon hot sauce and a pinch each of celery salt, black pepper and cayenne; toss with the chicken. Serve on buns with pimiento cheese and pickles.

**39. Tex-Mex Roll-Ups** Make Basic Poached Chicken (No. 34); shred. Mix with ⅔ cup mayonnaise, ½ cup salsa, ⅓ cup each sour cream, chopped canned green chiles and chopped scallions, and the juice of 1 lime. Serve in tortillas.

**40. Cheddar Melts** Make Basic Poached Chicken (No. 34); dice. Toss with ½ cup each diced celery and apple and 1 chopped scallion. Add 1 cup mayonnaise, 2 teaspoons mustard, and salt and pepper to taste. Spoon onto toasted English muffins; top with sliced cheddar and broil until melted.

**41. Basic Grilled** Season 4 small chicken breasts with salt and pepper. Grill on oiled grates over medium heat, turning once, 15 to 18 minutes.

**42. Tostadas** Make Basic Grilled Chicken (No. 41); slice. Mash 1 avocado with 2 tablespoons each sour cream and lime juice; season with salt and cayenne. Spread on 4 tostada shells. Top with the chicken, shredded lettuce, more sour cream and fresh salsa.

**43. Fajitas** Marinate 4 small chicken breasts in ¼ cup olive oil, the juice of 1 lime and 1 tablespoon each ground cumin, dried oregano and chili powder in the refrigerator, 30 minutes. Cook as for Basic Grilled Chicken (No. 41); slice. Grill 1 each sliced poblano and onion. Serve with the chicken in tortillas.

**44. Chipotle Barbecue** Puree ½ cup barbecue sauce with 1 chipotle in adobo. Make Basic Grilled Chicken (No. 41), brushing with the sauce during the last 5 minutes.

**45. Middle Eastern** Rub 4 small chicken breasts with a mixture of 1 tablespoon olive oil, 2 tablespoons pumpkin pie spice and ¼ teaspoon each cayenne and granulated garlic. Cook as for Basic Grilled Chicken (No. 41); serve with tzatziki and pita.

**46. Jerk Pineapple** Toss 4 small chicken breasts, 4 scallions, 2 sliced bell peppers and 1 sliced pineapple with vegetable oil and jerk seasoning. Cook as for Basic Grilled Chicken (No. 41), adding the pineapple and vegetables to the grill halfway through.

**47. Indian** Rub 4 small chicken breasts with 1½ teaspoons curry powder, and salt and pepper to taste. Cook as for Basic Grilled Chicken (No. 41). Puree ½ cup cilantro, ¼ cup each mint and coconut milk, 1 tablespoon lime juice, 1 teaspoon sugar, ½ jalapeño, 1 garlic clove and ¼ teaspoon kosher salt; serve with the chicken.

**48. Herb Oil** Marinate 4 small chicken breasts in ⅓ cup olive oil, the juice of 1 lemon and 1 teaspoon each kosher salt and red pepper flakes in the refrigerator, 1 hour. Cook as for Basic Grilled Chicken (No. 41). Puree ¼ cup each olive oil, fresh parsley and basil with 2 tablespoons lemon juice; season with salt and pepper. Serve the chicken with the sauce.

**49. Caesar Salad** Make Basic Grilled Chicken (No. 41) with 2 breasts; slice. Mash 1 minced garlic clove with 2 anchovies; mix with ¼ teaspoon Worcestershire sauce, the juice of ½ lemon and ½ cup mayonnaise. Toss with 1 head chopped romaine and the chicken. Top with grated parmesan.

**50. Pesto Panini** Make Basic Grilled Chicken (No. 41); slice. Sandwich between sliced Italian bread with pesto, sliced tomato and fresh mozzarella. Cook in a hot oiled skillet, 2 minutes per side.

# meat

# PORK WITH FENNEL AND POTATOES

ACTIVE: 20 min  I  TOTAL: 40 min  I  SERVES: 4

1½    pounds pork tenderloin (1 large or 2 small), trimmed
1½    teaspoons chopped fresh thyme
Kosher salt and freshly ground pepper
2    tablespoons extra-virgin olive oil
1    large fennel bulb, cut into wedges
4    cloves garlic, thinly sliced
1    pound small red-skinned potatoes, quartered
¼    cup dry white wine
¼    cup low-sodium chicken broth
½    cup heavy cream
2    tablespoons roughly chopped fresh parsley

**1.** Preheat the oven to 425°. Halve the pork tenderloin crosswise; sprinkle with 1 teaspoon thyme and ½ teaspoon each salt and pepper. Heat 1 tablespoon olive oil in a large nonstick skillet over medium-high heat. Add the pork and cook, turning, until browned, about 5 minutes. Transfer to a roasting pan; roast until a meat thermometer inserted into the thickest part of the pork registers 140°, 12 to 15 minutes.
**2.** Meanwhile, heat the remaining 1 tablespoon olive oil in a large saucepan over medium heat. Add the fennel, garlic, potatoes, wine and 1 cup water; season with salt and pepper. Stir, then cover and cook, stirring occasionally, until the potatoes are almost tender, 15 minutes.
**3.** Uncover and cook until the potatoes are tender, about 10 minutes. Add the broth and the remaining ½ teaspoon thyme. Simmer until slightly reduced, 1 minute. Add the cream; increase the heat and gently boil until slightly thickened, about 1 more minute. Season with salt and pepper. Slice the pork and serve with the vegetables and sauce. Top with parsley.

Per serving: Calories 482; Fat 24 g (Saturated 10 g); Cholesterol 137 mg; Sodium 366 mg; Carbohydrate 25 g; Fiber 4 g; Protein 38

# PORK CHOPS WITH CORN-BACON SLAW

ACTIVE: 20 min **I** TOTAL: 35 min **I** SERVES: 4

½    cup buttermilk
¼    cup mayonnaise
2    tablespoons chopped fresh parsley
2    tablespoons apple cider vinegar
1    clove garlic, grated
¼    teaspoon sugar
Kosher salt and freshly ground pepper
4    center-cut bone-in pork chops (½ to ¾ inch thick; 2 pounds)
4    slices bacon
2    ears of corn, kernels removed
4    cups shredded coleslaw mix
1    cup cherry tomatoes, halved

**1.** Preheat the broiler. Whisk the buttermilk, mayonnaise, parsley, vinegar, garlic, sugar, ¼ teaspoon salt, and pepper to taste in a medium bowl. Prick the pork chops all over with a fork. Set on a rimmed baking sheet, season with salt and pepper and drizzle with half of the buttermilk dressing, turning to coat. Let marinate 15 minutes at room temperature.
**2.** Transfer the baking sheet to the broiler and broil until the pork is browned, 4 to 5 minutes per side. Meanwhile, cook the bacon in a skillet over medium heat until crisp, 4 to 5 minutes per side. Remove to paper towels and let cool slightly; roughly chop. Add the corn to the drippings in the skillet and cook, stirring, until browned, about 3 minutes.
**3.** Combine the bacon, corn, coleslaw mix, tomatoes, ¼ teaspoon salt, and pepper to taste in a large bowl. Toss with the remaining buttermilk dressing. Brush the pork chops with any juices from the baking sheet; serve with the slaw.

Per serving: Calories 491; Fat 31 g (Saturated 10 g); Cholesterol 101 mg; Sodium 705 mg; Carbohydrate 20 g; Fiber 6 g; Protein 32 g

## GRILLED SAUSAGE KEBABS WITH PASTA SALAD

ACTIVE: 30 min I TOTAL: 30 min I SERVES: 4

Cooking spray
8    Italian sausage links (sweet, hot or a combination), halved crosswise
10   baby bell peppers (8 whole, 2 thinly sliced)
3    tablespoons extra-virgin olive oil
Kosher salt
1    cup pennette or other small pasta
2    cups baby spinach
¼    cup pitted green olives, sliced
1    clove garlic, grated or minced
2    tablespoons chopped fresh basil
Freshly ground pepper
2    tablespoons grated parmesan cheese

**1.** Heat a grill pan over medium heat and coat with cooking spray. Thread 2 sausage halves and 1 whole baby bell pepper onto each of 8 metal skewers. Brush the kebabs with 1 tablespoon olive oil and grill, turning as needed and covering the pan halfway through cooking, until marked all over, about 20 minutes.
**2.** Meanwhile, bring a large saucepan of salted water to a boil. Add the pasta and cook as the label directs. Combine the 2 sliced baby bell peppers, the spinach, olives, garlic, basil and the remaining 2 tablespoons olive oil in a large bowl; toss to coat. Drain the pasta and immediately transfer to the bowl with the spinach mixture; toss to combine. Season with salt and pepper and top with the cheese. Serve the pasta salad with the kebabs.

Per serving: Calories 493; Fat 26 g (Saturated 7 g); Cholesterol 48 mg; Sodium 944 mg; Carbohydrate 36 g; Fiber 3 g; Protein 30 g

# HOISIN PORK WITH RICE

ACTIVE: 25 min **I** TOTAL: 30 min **I** SERVES: 4

¼ cup hoisin sauce
2 tablespoons plus 1 teaspoon rice vinegar (not seasoned)
½ jalapeño pepper (seeded for less heat)
4 scallions, sliced
Freshly ground pepper
1 ¾-pound pork tenderloin, trimmed
Kosher salt
1½ pounds frozen brown rice (about 5 cups)
4 ounces snow peas, trimmed and halved
1 tablespoon plus 1 teaspoon extra-virgin olive oil
1 tablespoon grated peeled ginger
2 teaspoons toasted sesame seeds
2 medium carrots, shredded

**1.** Preheat the broiler. Combine the hoisin sauce, 1 tablespoon vinegar, the jalapeño, half of the scallions and ¼ teaspoon pepper in a blender or mini food processor and pulse until smooth. Transfer to a bowl.
**2.** Slice the pork tenderloin in half lengthwise and place both pieces cut-side down on a baking sheet. Sprinkle with ¼ teaspoon salt and brush with half of the hoisin sauce mixture. Broil until golden brown and just cooked through, 5 to 8 minutes. Set aside.
**3.** Combine the frozen rice, snow peas, 1 tablespoon each olive oil and vinegar, the ginger, 1 teaspoon sesame seeds and ¼ teaspoon salt in a microwave-safe bowl. Cover with plastic wrap and microwave until the rice is hot and the snow peas are tender, 6 to 8 minutes.
**4.** Toss the carrots, the remaining scallions and 1 teaspoon each olive oil, vinegar and sesame seeds in a bowl. Thinly slice the pork; serve with the rice mixture, carrot salad and remaining sauce.

Per serving: Calories 480; Fat 11 g (Saturated 2 g); Cholesterol 47 mg; Sodium 854 mg; Carbohydrate 72 g; Fiber 7 g; Protein 25 g

## KIELBASA WITH MASHED POTATOES
ACTIVE: 30 min **I** TOTAL: 40 min **I** SERVES: 4

1½    pounds small Yukon gold potatoes, halved
1      pound kielbasa
1½    tablespoons unsalted butter
1      small head broccoli, florets roughly chopped
1      cup sauerkraut, drained
⅔    cup whole milk
1      tablespoon whole-grain mustard
Kosher salt and freshly ground pepper

**1.** Put the potatoes in a large microwave-safe bowl and add 3 tablespoons water; cover with plastic wrap and microwave until tender, about 12 minutes.
**2.** Meanwhile, cut the kielbasa into 4 equal pieces; halve lengthwise. Melt ½ tablespoon butter in a large skillet over medium heat. Add the kielbasa and cook, turning occasionally, until browned and heated through, about 10 minutes. Transfer to a plate and cover loosely with foil to keep warm.
**3.** Increase the heat under the skillet to medium high; add the remaining 1 tablespoon butter. Add the broccoli and ¼ cup water and cook, stirring, until crisp-tender, about 5 minutes. Add the sauerkraut and toss to warm through.
**4.** Drain the potatoes. Warm the milk in the microwave, about 1 minute; add to the potatoes along with the mustard, ½ teaspoon salt, and pepper to taste. Coarsely mash with a potato masher or fork. Serve the kielbasa with the potatoes and the broccoli.

Per serving: Calories 491; Fat 26 g (Saturated 11 g); Cholesterol 95 mg; Sodium 1,850 mg; Carbohydrate 42 g; Fiber 5 g; Protein 23 g

LOW-CALORIE DINNER

# MEXICAN EGGS WITH CHORIZO AND BEANS

ACTIVE: 30 min **I** TOTAL: 30 min **I** SERVES: 4

- 2 ounces dried chorizo, diced (about 1 small link)
- 1 medium red bell pepper, chopped
- 1 jalapeño pepper, chopped (remove seeds for less heat)
- 1 14-ounce can no-salt-added pinto beans, drained and rinsed
- 3 scallions, sliced
- 6 large eggs plus 2 egg whites

Kosher salt and freshly ground pepper

- 1 cup crushed baked tortilla chips (preferably low sodium)
- ¾ cup shredded low-fat cheddar cheese (about 3 ounces)
- 2 tablespoons chopped fresh cilantro
- 1 avocado, pitted, peeled and sliced
- 2 tablespoons low-fat sour cream

**1.** Cook the chorizo in a large nonstick skillet over medium heat until it just begins to brown, about 3 minutes. Add the bell pepper and jalapeño and cook, stirring occasionally, until they begin to sizzle, about 5 minutes. Add the beans and half of the scallions and cook, stirring occasionally, until heated through, about 4 minutes.
**2.** Whisk the whole eggs and egg whites with ¼ cup water and ⅛ teaspoon each salt and pepper in a bowl; add to the skillet and cook, stirring with a rubber spatula, until just beginning to set, about 2 minutes. Add the chips, cheese, half of the cilantro, and the remaining scallions and continue cooking, stirring, until the eggs are just set, about 3 more minutes.
**3.** Divide the eggs among plates and top with the avocado, sour cream and remaining cilantro.

Per serving: Calories 406; Fat 20 g (Saturated 7 g); Cholesterol 349 mg; Sodium 426 mg; Carbohydrate 30 g; Fiber 9 g; Protein 29 g

# PORK CHOPS WITH BEAN SALAD

ACTIVE: 30 min I TOTAL: 40 min I SERVES: 4

3    tablespoons white wine vinegar
1½   teaspoons sugar
Kosher salt and freshly ground pepper
4    boneless pork loin chops (1¼ to 1½ pounds), trimmed
½    pound mixed green and wax beans, trimmed and cut into pieces
1    small red bell pepper, thinly sliced
¾    cup frozen corn
1    15-ounce can kidney beans, drained and rinsed
2    tablespoons extra-virgin olive oil
1    large shallot or ½ medium red onion, thinly sliced
¼    cup chopped fresh parsley
2    teaspoons dijon mustard

**1.** Whisk 2 cups cold water, 1 tablespoon vinegar, 1 teaspoon each sugar and salt, and pepper to taste in a bowl. Prick the pork a few times with a fork, then soak in the brine 15 minutes; remove and pat dry.
**2.** Meanwhile, bring a saucepan of salted water to a boil. Add the green and wax beans and cook until crisp-tender, 4 minutes. Add the bell pepper and corn; cook 1 minute. Drain the vegetables, rinse under cold water and pat dry. Transfer to a bowl and add the kidney beans.
**3.** Season the pork with salt and pepper. Heat 1 tablespoon olive oil in a nonstick skillet over medium-high heat. Add the pork and cook until golden, about 4 minutes per side; transfer to a plate.
**4.** Wipe out the skillet; heat the remaining 1 tablespoon olive oil over medium heat. Add the shallot and cook 3 minutes. Add the remaining 2 tablespoons vinegar and cook until absorbed. Whisk in ½ cup water, half of the parsley, the mustard, the remaining ½ teaspoon sugar, and salt to taste. Simmer 3 minutes, then toss with the vegetables. Add the remaining parsley and season with salt and pepper. Serve with the pork chops.

Per serving: Calories 370; Fat 12 g (Saturated 3 g); Cholesterol 79 mg; Sodium 276 mg; Carbohydrate 28 g; Fiber 12 g; Protein 37 g

# PORK CHOPS WITH PINEAPPLE SALSA

ACTIVE: 20 min **I** TOTAL: 35 min **I** SERVES: 4

1    cup medium- or long-grain white rice
1    pineapple, peeled, quartered lengthwise and cored
1    tablespoon minced peeled ginger
1    tablespoon vegetable oil
1    tablespoon soy sauce, plus a splash for the salsa
½    teaspoon Chinese five-spice powder
1    bunch scallions
4    bone-in pork sirloin chops (½ inch thick; about 1¾ pounds)
Pinch of red pepper flakes

**1.** Combine the rice and 1⅔ cups water in a medium saucepan and bring to a boil. Cover, reduce the heat to low and cook until the rice is tender and the water is absorbed, about 15 minutes. Remove from the heat and let stand until ready to serve.
**2.** Meanwhile, cut off a 2-inch piece of the pineapple and grate it on the coarse holes of a box grater into a large bowl. Stir in the ginger, vegetable oil, 1 tablespoon soy sauce and ¼ teaspoon five-spice powder. Add the scallions and pork chops and turn to coat; let marinate at room temperature, 10 minutes. Rub the remaining pineapple with the remaining ¼ teaspoon five-spice powder.
**3.** Preheat a grill to medium high. Grill the pork chops until just cooked through, about 3 minutes per side. Grill the scallions and pineapple, turning occasionally, until charred, about 3 minutes.
**4.** Roughly chop the pineapple and scallions and transfer to a bowl. Add the red pepper flakes and a splash of soy sauce and toss. Serve the pork chops with the pineapple salsa and rice.

Per serving: Calories 484; Fat 16 g (Saturated 5 g); Cholesterol 71 mg; Sodium 209 mg; Carbohydrate 58 g; Fiber 3 g; Protein 27 g

# PORK AND NOODLE STIR-FRY

ACTIVE: 30 min **I** TOTAL: 35 min **I** SERVES: 4

8    ounces rice noodles
1    pork tenderloin (about ¾ pound), cut into ¼-inch-thick strips
Kosher salt and freshly ground pepper
3    tablespoons cornstarch
2    cups fat-free low-sodium chicken broth
4    teaspoons vegetable oil
4    scallions, sliced (white and green parts separated)
1    2-inch piece ginger, peeled and minced
2    cloves garlic, minced
3    cups precut stir-fry vegetables (about 9 ounces)
Grated zest of 1 lime, plus wedges for serving

**1.** Cook the noodles as the label directs, then drain and rinse under cold water. Meanwhile, toss the pork with ¼ teaspoon salt, pepper to taste and 2 tablespoons cornstarch in a bowl. Whisk the chicken broth and the remaining 1 tablespoon cornstarch in another bowl.
**2.** Heat a large nonstick skillet over high heat. Add 1 teaspoon vegetable oil, then add the pork and stir-fry until lightly browned, about 5 minutes; transfer to a bowl. Add the remaining 3 teaspoons vegetable oil to the pan, then add the scallion whites, ginger and garlic; reduce the heat to medium and cook, stirring occasionally, 2 minutes. Stir in the vegetables and 3 tablespoons water and cook, stirring occasionally, until the vegetables are crisp-tender, about 4 minutes. Add the broth mixture to the pan and bring to a boil; cook, stirring occasionally, until slightly thickened, about 5 minutes.
**3.** Return the pork to the skillet along with the noodles, lime zest and ¼ teaspoon salt and stir to heat through. Stir in the scallion greens. Divide among bowls and serve with lime wedges.

Per serving: Calories 415; Fat 9 g (Saturated 2 g); Cholesterol 68 mg; Sodium 465 mg; Carbohydrate 59 g; Fiber 3 g; Protein 24 g

# PORK CHOPS SALTIMBOCCA

ACTIVE: 35 min **I** TOTAL: 40 min **I** SERVES: 4

4  7-to-8-ounce boneless center-cut pork chops (about ¾ inch thick)
Kosher salt and freshly ground pepper
4  large sage leaves
8  thin slices prosciutto
3  tablespoons extra-virgin olive oil
4  slices provolone cheese (about 3½ ounces)
1  pound baby spinach
Juice of 1 lemon, plus wedges for serving
1  large shallot, finely chopped, or ⅓ cup finely chopped red onion
⅔  cup low-sodium chicken broth

**1.** Preheat the oven to 425°. Season the pork with salt and pepper. Top each chop with a sage leaf, then wrap in 2 slices prosciutto.
**2.** Heat 2 tablespoons olive oil in a large skillet over medium-high heat. Add the chops, sage-side down, and cook, turning once, until the prosciutto is crisp, 8 to 10 minutes. Transfer to a baking sheet, reserving the skillet, and roast until a thermometer inserted sideways into the center of a chop registers 145°, about 8 minutes. Top each with a slice of provolone; return to the oven until the cheese melts, 1 to 2 minutes.
**3.** Meanwhile, put the spinach in a microwave-safe bowl; add the remaining 1 tablespoon olive oil, 1 tablespoon water and a pinch of salt. Cover with plastic wrap and microwave until wilted, 3 minutes; drain. Drizzle with half of the lemon juice and season with salt and pepper.
**4.** Heat the reserved skillet over medium heat; add the shallot and cook, stirring, until soft, 3 minutes. Add the broth and simmer until reduced by half. Stir in the remaining lemon juice and season with salt and pepper. Divide the pork among plates; drizzle with the shallot sauce. Serve with the spinach and lemon wedges.

Per serving: Calories 583; Fat 37 g (Saturated 13 g); Cholesterol 143 mg;
Sodium 1,330 mg; Carbohydrate 16 g; Fiber 5 g; Protein 48 g

## PORK SCALLOPINI SALAD
ACTIVE: 25 min  |  TOTAL: 35 min  |  SERVES: 4

Juice of 1 lemon
2      tablespoons red wine vinegar
1      small shallot, chopped
3      tablespoons extra-virgin olive oil, plus more for drizzling
1½    teaspoons chopped fresh rosemary
Kosher salt and freshly ground pepper
1¼    pounds pork scallopini
1      pint grape tomatoes, halved
5      radishes, thinly sliced
Vegetable oil, for the grill
4      pieces lavash or pita bread
8      ounces mixed salad greens (about 8 cups)
2      ounces gruyère cheese, thinly sliced

**1.** Whisk the lemon juice, vinegar, shallot, olive oil, rosemary, ¼ teaspoon salt, and pepper to taste in a large bowl. Transfer 3 tablespoons of the dressing to a medium bowl and add the pork, turning to coat; let marinate 15 minutes at room temperature. Add the tomatoes and radishes to the bowl with the remaining dressing.
**2.** Preheat a grill or grill pan to high and brush lightly with vegetable oil. Grill the pork until marked, about 2 minutes per side; remove to a plate. Grill the bread, turning once, until warm, about 1 minute.
**3.** Add the salad greens to the bowl with the tomatoes and radishes; season with salt and pepper and toss. Divide the salad among plates; top with the gruyère and pork. Drizzle with olive oil and serve with the grilled bread.

Per serving: Calories 495; Fat 26 g (Saturated 8 g); Cholesterol 107 mg; Sodium 410 mg; Carbohydrate 26 g; Fiber 4 g; Protein 40 g

# PORK TENDERLOIN WITH APPLES
ACTIVE: 20 min | TOTAL: 40 min | SERVES: 4

1     large pork tenderloin (about 1¼ pounds)
¼     teaspoon pumpkin pie spice
Kosher salt and freshly ground pepper
1     tablespoon extra-virgin olive oil
2     baking apples (such as McIntosh)
1½    tablespoons unsalted butter
1     medium shallot, finely chopped
1     cup quick-cooking barley
1     tablespoon finely chopped fresh parsley
¼     cup apple cider
1     tablespoon apple cider vinegar

**1.** Preheat the oven to 400°. Sprinkle the pork with the pumpkin pie spice, ½ teaspoon salt, and pepper to taste. Heat the olive oil in a large ovenproof skillet over medium-high heat. Add the pork and cook, turning, until browned on all sides, about 6 minutes.
**2.** Halve the apples and scoop out the cores. Cut ½ tablespoon butter into 4 pieces; put a piece in each apple half. Sprinkle with half of the shallot and a pinch of salt. Add the apples to the skillet with the pork, cut-side up, and transfer to the oven. Roast until a meat thermometer registers 145°, about 25 minutes.
**3.** Meanwhile, combine 1¾ cups water, the remaining shallot and a pinch of salt in a saucepan; bring to a boil. Add the barley, cover and cook over low heat until the water is absorbed, 12 minutes. Add the parsley.
**4.** Transfer the pork and apples to a cutting board. Return the skillet to medium-high heat and add the cider, vinegar and ¼ cup water; simmer, stirring, 2 minutes. Stir in the remaining 1 tablespoon butter. Slice the pork and serve with the pan sauce, apples and barley.

Per serving: Calories 474; Fat 14 g (Saturated 5 g); Cholesterol 103 mg;
Sodium 318 mg; Carbohydrate 53 g; Fiber 10 g; Protein 35 g

# WESTERN HASH BROWN OMELET

ACTIVE: 35 min **I** TOTAL: 40 min **I** SERVES: 4

Kids'
MEAL

| | |
|---|---|
| 8 | large eggs |
| 2 | tablespoons extra-virgin olive oil |
| 4 | ounces thickly sliced deli ham, diced |
| 2 | bell peppers (1 red, 1 green), diced |
| 1 | onion, diced |

Kosher salt and freshly ground pepper

| | |
|---|---|
| 2 | tablespoons unsalted butter |
| 3 | cups frozen shredded hash browns (from a 1-pound bag; do not thaw) |
| 4 | ounces smoked gouda cheese, grated (about 1½ cups) |
| 1 | bunch scallions, chopped |

**1.** Beat the eggs in a large bowl until foamy. Heat the olive oil in a large nonstick ovenproof skillet over medium-high heat. Add the ham, bell peppers, onion, ¼ teaspoon salt and a few grinds of pepper. Cook, stirring occasionally, until the vegetables are tender and starting to brown, about 6 minutes; add to the bowl with the eggs.
**2.** Preheat the broiler. Wipe out the skillet and return to medium-high heat. Melt the butter in the skillet, then add the frozen hash browns in an even layer. Cook, pressing the hash browns into the bottom and up the side of the skillet with a spatula, until golden on the bottom, about 6 minutes.
**3.** Pour the egg mixture over the hash browns. Transfer the skillet to the broiler; cook until partially set, 3 to 5 minutes. Sprinkle the cheese and all but about 2 tablespoons scallions over the eggs. Continue broiling until the cheese melts and the eggs are set, 2 to 3 more minutes.
**4.** Loosen the edge of the omelet with a small spatula. Slide onto a platter and fold in half. Cut into wedges; top with the reserved scallions.

Per serving: Calories 474; Fat 30 g (Saturated 13 g); Cholesterol 490 mg;
Sodium 914 mg; Carbohydrate 26 g; Fiber 7 g; Protein 28 g

# PORK TACOS WITH BLACK BEANS

ACTIVE: 30 min **I** TOTAL: 30 min **I** SERVES: 4

| | |
|---|---|
| 2½ | tablespoons vegetable oil |
| 2 | cloves garlic, minced |
| 1 | 15-ounce can black beans (do not drain) |
| ½ | cup shredded mozzarella cheese (about 2 ounces) |
| 1 | pound ground pork |
| 1 | small red onion, finely chopped |
| 1 | teaspoon ground cumin |
| ½ | teaspoon cayenne pepper |

Kosher salt

| | |
|---|---|
| 1 | bell pepper (any color), cut into ½-inch pieces |
| 1 | zucchini, quartered and cut into ½-inch pieces |

Freshly ground black pepper

12   corn tortillas, warmed

**1.** Heat ½ tablespoon vegetable oil in a small saucepan over medium heat. Add half of the garlic and cook, stirring, until golden, about 1 minute. Add the beans and bring to a simmer. Remove from the heat, sprinkle with the cheese and cover to keep warm.

**2.** Heat 1 tablespoon vegetable oil in a skillet over medium-high heat. Add the pork, the remaining garlic, half of the red onion, the cumin, cayenne and ½ teaspoon salt. Cook, stirring, until the pork is browned, about 5 minutes; transfer to a bowl with a slotted spoon. Heat the remaining 1 tablespoon vegetable oil in the skillet. Add the bell pepper, zucchini and ¼ teaspoon salt and cook until crisp-tender, about 3 minutes. Return the pork to the skillet; add a splash of water, and salt and pepper to taste.

**3.** Fill the tortillas with the pork and vegetable mixture. Serve with the beans. Sprinkle with the remaining chopped onion.

Per serving: Calories 616; Fat 38 g (Saturated 12 g); Cholesterol 89 mg; Sodium 596 mg; Carbohydrate 39 g; Fiber 6 g; Protein 33 g

DONE IN
**25**
MINUTES

## BISTRO CHEF'S SALAD
ACTIVE: 25 min **I** TOTAL: 25 min **I** SERVES: 4

2    tablespoons white wine vinegar
4    ounces brie cheese, sliced
2    6-inch baguette segments, split and toasted
⅓    cup sliced fresh basil
1    tablespoon dijon mustard
Kosher salt and freshly ground pepper
¼    cup extra-virgin olive oil
4    large eggs
1    5-ounce package mixed baby greens
1    small head frisée, torn into bite-size pieces
1    large tomato, cut into wedges
½    pound thickly sliced Black Forest ham, cut into strips

**1.** Fill a wide, shallow pot with 2 inches of water. Add ½ tablespoon vinegar and bring
to a gentle simmer.
**2.** Meanwhile, divide the brie between the baguette pieces and sprinkle with about
1 tablespoon of the basil. Whisk the mustard, the remaining 1½ tablespoons vinegar,
½ teaspoon salt, and pepper to taste in a large bowl. Slowly whisk in the olive oil
until smooth.
**3.** One at a time, crack each egg into a small bowl or cup, then slip into the simmering
water. Poach the eggs until the whites are set but the yolks are still runny, 2 to 3 minutes.
Using a slotted spoon, transfer the eggs to a paper towel–lined plate to drain briefly.
**4.** Add the mixed greens, frisée and the remaining basil to the bowl with the dressing and
toss; season with salt and pepper. Divide among plates and top with the tomato and ham.
Season the eggs with salt and pepper and add to the salads. Serve with the baguette pieces.

Per serving: Calories 513; Fat 30 g (Saturated 9 g); Cholesterol 265 mg;
Sodium 1,346 mg; Carbohydrate 34 g; Fiber 2 g; Protein 26 g

## STIR-FRY FRITTATA

ACTIVE: 20 min I TOTAL: 40 min I SERVES: 4

1    12-to-16-ounce bag frozen stir-fry vegetables
½    cup fresh cilantro (leaves and tender stems), plus more for topping
Grated zest and juice of 1 lime
3    tablespoons peanut or vegetable oil
1    1-inch piece ginger, peeled
1    large clove garlic
½    jalapeño pepper (remove seeds for less heat)
3    teaspoons hoisin sauce, plus more for topping
10   large eggs
Kosher salt and freshly ground pepper
½    pound ground pork

**1.** Preheat the oven to 400°. Put the vegetables in a microwave-safe bowl and cover with plastic wrap; microwave until warmed through, about 4 minutes. Drain and set aside.
**2.** Combine the cilantro, lime zest and juice, 2 tablespoons water, 1 tablespoon peanut oil, the ginger, garlic, jalapeño and 2 teaspoons hoisin sauce in a blender; puree until smooth. Whisk the eggs, 2 tablespoons water, ½ teaspoon salt, and pepper to taste in a large bowl.
**3.** Heat the remaining 2 tablespoons peanut oil in a medium ovenproof nonstick skillet over medium-high heat. Add the pork, the remaining 1 teaspoon hoisin sauce, and ¼ teaspoon salt; cook, stirring, until browned, 4 minutes. Stir in the vegetables, half of the cilantro-ginger sauce, and salt and pepper to taste. Pour in the eggs, increase the heat to high and cook 2 minutes.
**4.** Transfer the skillet to the oven and bake until set, 20 to 25 minutes. Cover and let rest 5 minutes. Top with the remaining cilantro-ginger sauce, more hoisin sauce and cilantro.

Per serving: Calories 461; Fat 34 g (Saturated 10 g); Cholesterol 578 mg;
Sodium 831 mg; Carbohydrate 14 g; Fiber 3 g; Protein 27 g

# HAM AND VEGETABLE GRATIN

ACTIVE: 25 min **I** TOTAL: 40 min **I** SERVES: 4

| | |
|---|---|
| 4 | tablespoons unsalted butter |
| 1 | small onion, chopped |
| 2 | large Yukon gold potatoes (about 1 pound), diced |
| 1 | 10-ounce package frozen mixed peas and carrots |
| ¼ | pound low-sodium ham, chopped (about ¾ cup) |
| 3 | tablespoons whole-wheat flour |
| ½ | teaspoon dried thyme |
| 1½ | cups fat-free low-sodium chicken broth |
| ⅔ | cup low-fat (2%) milk |
| ¾ | cup panko breadcrumbs |
| 2 | tablespoons chopped fresh parsley |

Kosher salt and freshly ground pepper

**1.** Preheat the oven to 375°. Melt 1 tablespoon butter in a large ovenproof skillet over medium-high heat. Add the onion, potatoes and frozen peas and carrots and cook, stirring occasionally, until the vegetables begin to soften, about 5 minutes. Add the ham, flour and thyme and cook, stirring, until combined. Stir in the chicken broth and bring to a boil, then stir in the milk and simmer until slightly thickened, about 3 minutes. Transfer the skillet to the oven and bake until the potatoes are tender, about 20 minutes.

**2.** Meanwhile, melt the remaining 3 tablespoons butter in a medium skillet over medium-high heat. Add the panko, parsley and ⅛ teaspoon each salt and pepper and cook, stirring occasionally, until the panko is slightly toasted, about 4 minutes. Scatter over the ham and vegetable mixture; let rest 5 minutes before serving.

Per serving: Calories 392; Fat 14 g (Saturated 8 g); Cholesterol 41 mg; Sodium 710 mg; Carbohydrate 51 g; Fiber 5 g; Protein 15 g

## ASIAN STEAK FRITES
ACTIVE: 40 min **I** TOTAL: 40 min **I** SERVES: 4

1    20-ounce package frozen french fries
¼    teaspoon Chinese five-spice powder
Kosher salt
¾    cup ketchup
3    tablespoons sweet pickle relish
2    tablespoons Sriracha (Asian chile sauce)
1¼   pounds flank steak
1    tablespoon vegetable oil, plus more for brushing
1    English cucumber, peeled and cut into ¾-inch pieces
1    tablespoon rice vinegar (not seasoned)
Freshly ground pepper
3    scallions, thinly sliced

**1.** Toss the fries with ⅛ teaspoon five-spice powder and ½ teaspoon salt on a baking sheet; bake as the label directs until crisp.
**2.** Meanwhile, preheat a grill pan over high heat. Mix the ketchup, relish, Sriracha and the remaining ⅛ teaspoon five-spice powder in a bowl; set aside 2 tablespoons for brushing the steak.
**3.** Prick the steak all over with a fork; season with salt. Brush the grill pan with oil, then add the steak and grill until marked, 12 to 15 minutes, flipping and brushing occasionally with the reserved spiced ketchup. Transfer to a cutting board; let rest 10 minutes, then thinly slice against the grain.
**4.** Toss the cucumber, vegetable oil and vinegar in a bowl; season with salt and pepper. Toss the fries with the scallions, and salt to taste. Serve with the steak and the spiced ketchup.

Per serving: Calories 534; Fat 19 g (Saturated 4 g); Cholesterol 54 mg; Sodium 1,342 mg; Carbohydrate 55 g; Fiber 5 g; Protein 34 g

# SKIRT STEAK WITH PEPPERS

ACTIVE: 30 min ❙ TOTAL: 30 min ❙ SERVES: 4

LOW-
CALORIE
DINNER

1 pound baby red-skinned potatoes, halved
Kosher salt
1¼ pounds skirt steak
Freshly ground pepper
1 tablespoon extra-virgin olive oil
3 bell peppers (any color), thinly sliced
½ onion, thinly sliced
2 cloves garlic, thinly sliced
3 tablespoons tomato paste
3 tablespoons chopped fresh parsley
Juice of ½ lemon, plus wedges for serving

**1.** Put the potatoes in a pot and cover with cold water by about 1 inch; add salt. Bring to a simmer and cook until fork-tender, about 8 minutes, then drain.
**2.** Meanwhile, cut the steak crosswise into 8 pieces and season with salt and pepper. Heat a large skillet over medium-high heat and add the olive oil. When hot, add the steak (in batches, if necessary) and cook until medium rare, 1 to 5 minutes per side, depending on the thickness. Transfer to a plate and tent loosely with aluminum foil.
**3.** Reduce the heat under the skillet to medium and add the bell peppers, onion, garlic, a splash of water and ¼ teaspoon salt; cook, stirring often, until the vegetables are slightly soft, about 5 minutes. Add the tomato paste and cook, stirring, 1 minute. Increase the heat to medium high, add ¾ cup water and simmer until the vegetables are tender, about 4 more minutes. Stir in the potatoes, parsley and lemon juice. Divide the steak among plates and serve with the vegetables and lemon wedges.

Per serving: Calories 449; Fat 23 g (Saturated 8 g); Cholesterol 75 mg;
Sodium 323 mg; Carbohydrate 29 g; Fiber 5 g; Protein 31 g

# LONDON BROIL WITH CHEESY YORKSHIRE PUDDING

ACTIVE: 25 min **I** TOTAL: 40 min **I** SERVES: 4

1½ pounds top round steak (London broil)
2 teaspoons Worcestershire sauce
Kosher salt and freshly ground pepper
3 large eggs
1 cup whole milk
1 cup all-purpose flour
2 scallions, chopped
½ cup grated sharp cheddar cheese (about 2 ounces)
2 tablespoons unsalted butter, melted
½ tablespoon vegetable oil
3 plum tomatoes, quartered

**1.** Preheat the oven to 450°. Rub the steak with the Worcestershire sauce, ½ teaspoon salt and a generous amount of pepper; set aside.
**2.** Make the Yorkshire pudding: Whisk the eggs and milk in a large bowl; add the flour, scallions, cheese and ½ teaspoon salt and whisk to combine. Lightly brush a deep-dish pie plate with some of the butter, then whisk the remaining butter into the batter. Pour the batter into the prepared pie plate and bake until puffed and golden, 20 to 25 minutes.
**3.** Meanwhile, heat the vegetable oil in a large skillet over medium heat until very hot. Add the steak and cook until browned on the bottom, about 5 minutes. Flip the steak, reduce the heat to low and cover the skillet; continue cooking until a thermometer inserted sideways into the center of the steak registers 120°, 10 to 12 minutes. Transfer to a cutting board, tent with foil and let rest, 10 minutes. Add the tomatoes to the skillet, cut-side down; cover and cook until soft, 5 minutes.
**4.** Thinly slice the steak against the grain and season with pepper. Cut the Yorkshire pudding into wedges. Serve with the tomatoes.

Per serving: Calories 567; Fat 28 g (Saturated 14 g); Cholesterol 262 mg; Sodium 741 mg; Carbohydrate 28 g; Fiber 1 g; Protein 48 g

## SKILLET BEEF PIE
ACTIVE: 25 min I TOTAL: 40 min I SERVES: 4

2    tablespoons vegetable oil
1    large onion, finely chopped
1    large red bell pepper, finely chopped
4    cloves garlic, finely chopped
Kosher salt and freshly ground pepper
1    14.5-ounce can diced tomatoes with green chiles
2    teaspoons ground cumin
½    teaspoon ground cinnamon
1    pound ground beef chuck
½    cup golden raisins
½    cup chopped pimiento-stuffed olives
1    piece refrigerated pie dough (half of a 14-ounce package)

**1.** Preheat the oven to 425°. Heat the vegetable oil in a 10-inch ovenproof skillet over medium-high heat. Add the onion, bell pepper, garlic and a generous pinch each of salt and pepper. Cook, stirring occasionally, until the vegetables are lightly browned and just tender, about 6 minutes. Add the tomatoes, cumin and cinnamon and cook, stirring occasionally, until thickened, about 5 minutes.
**2.** Push the vegetables to one side of the skillet and add the beef to the other side; season the beef with salt and pepper. Increase the heat to high and cook, stirring the ingredients together, until the beef is no longer pink, about 3 minutes. Stir in the raisins and olives and remove from the heat.
**3.** Unroll the pie crust and center it over the filling; press the edge against the inside of the skillet using a fork. Transfer to the oven and bake until the crust is golden brown, 15 to 20 minutes.

Per serving: Calories 610; Fat 35 g (Saturated 12 g); Cholesterol 79 mg;
Sodium 891 mg; Carbohydrate 52 g; Fiber 4 g; Protein 24 g

Kids'
MEAL

# GRILLED CHEESY MEATLOAVES
ACTIVE: 15 min **I** TOTAL: 30 min **I** SERVES: 4

| | |
|---|---|
| 1 | bunch scallions (white and light green parts), cut into pieces |
| 1 | stalk celery, cut into pieces |
| ¼ | cup fresh parsley |
| 1 | pound 90% lean ground beef sirloin |
| 1 | cup panko breadcrumbs |
| 1 | large egg |
| 2 | teaspoons Worcestershire sauce, plus more for brushing |

Kosher salt and freshly ground pepper

| | |
|---|---|
| 3 | ounces sharp cheddar cheese, cut into four 2-inch-long sticks |

Cooking spray

| | |
|---|---|
| 3 | assorted bell peppers, quartered or cut into large chunks |
| ¼ | cup ketchup |

**1.** Preheat a grill to medium high. Pulse the scallions, celery and parsley in a food processor until finely chopped; transfer to a bowl. Add the beef, panko, egg, 2 teaspoons Worcestershire sauce, ½ teaspoon salt, and pepper to taste. Mix with your hands, then divide into 4 portions; set a piece of cheese on each. Mold the beef around the cheese and form into mini oval-shaped loaves.
**2.** Stack 2 large sheets of heavy-duty foil; coat the top sheet with cooking spray. Arrange the meatloaves 1½ inches apart in the center of the foil; coat with cooking spray. Bring the foil edges together to make a packet and crimp to seal. Set the packet seam-side down on the grill; add the peppers to the grill, skin-side down. Cover and cook 10 minutes. Flip the peppers, brush with Worcestershire sauce and sprinkle with salt; flip the packet. Continue cooking, covered, 5 to 8 more minutes.
**3.** Remove the peppers and packet from the grill. Brush the meatloaves with ketchup. Return the open packet to the grill; cook 5 more minutes.

Per serving: Calories 314; Fat 12 g (Saturated 6 g); Cholesterol 104 mg; Sodium 748 mg; Carbohydrate 25 g; Fiber 3 g; Protein 28 g

# LIGHT SHEPHERD'S PIE
ACTIVE: 30 min **I** TOTAL: 35 min **I** SERVES: 4

LOW-CALORIE DINNER

1¼   pounds small red-skinned potatoes
2   tablespoons extra-virgin olive oil
1   small onion, finely chopped
1   carrot, finely chopped
2   large tomatoes, chopped
1½   tablespoons chili powder
Kosher salt
½   pound 93% lean ground turkey
½   pound 90% lean ground beef sirloin
1½   cups frozen peas
½   cup low-fat milk, warmed
⅓   cup shredded low-fat cheddar cheese

**1.** Put the potatoes in a microwave-safe bowl and add 2 tablespoons water; cover and microwave until tender, 8 to 10 minutes. Let stand, covered, until ready to mash. Meanwhile, heat 1 tablespoon olive oil in a large skillet over medium-high heat. Add the onion, carrot, tomatoes, ¾ teaspoon chili powder and ½ teaspoon salt; cover and cook, stirring occasionally, until the vegetables are tender, about 10 minutes. Transfer to a 2-quart baking dish.
**2.** Heat the remaining 1 tablespoon olive oil in the skillet over medium-high heat. Add the turkey, beef, the remaining ¾ teaspoon chili powder and ½ teaspoon salt; cook, stirring and breaking up the meat with a wooden spoon, until browned, about 4 minutes. Stir in the peas and ¼ cup water; simmer 2 minutes. Spread over the vegetables in the baking dish, then cover to keep warm.
**3.** Preheat the broiler. Add the milk and ¼ teaspoon salt to the potatoes and mash well; mix in the cheese. Spread over the meat and broil until browned in spots, 1 to 2 minutes.

Per serving: Calories 448; Fat 19 g (Saturated 6 g); Cholesterol 77 mg; Sodium 847 mg; Carbohydrate 38 g; Fiber 6 g; Protein 32 g

## MIDDLE EASTERN STEAK PITAS
ACTIVE: 35 min I TOTAL: 40 min I SERVES: 4

1¼  pounds flank steak, thinly sliced against the grain
1    medium onion, thinly sliced
1    teaspoon pumpkin pie spice
¼    cup fresh lemon juice
3    tablespoons extra-virgin olive oil
2    cloves garlic, minced
¼    cup chopped fresh parsley and/or mint
Kosher salt and freshly ground pepper
¼    cup tahini (sesame paste)
2    medium tomatoes, diced
3    small Persian cucumbers, peeled and chopped
4    pocketless pitas

**1.** Combine the steak, onion, pumpkin pie spice, 2 tablespoons lemon juice,
1 tablespoon olive oil, 1 minced garlic clove, 2 tablespoons chopped herbs,
1 teaspoon salt and ½ teaspoon pepper in a bowl; toss well to coat. Set aside
while you prepare the salad.
**2.** Whisk the tahini, the remaining garlic and 2 tablespoons lemon juice, and
1 tablespoon olive oil in a separate bowl; stir in the tomatoes and cucumbers.
**3.** Heat a cast-iron skillet over medium-high heat until very hot. Brush the pitas
with the remaining 1 tablespoon olive oil; cook until lightly toasted, about 1 minute
per side. Transfer to plates. Working in batches, add the meat and onion to
the skillet in a single layer and cook until browned, about 2 minutes per side.
**4.** Serve the steak and onion on the pitas with the cucumber salad. Top with the
remaining herbs.

Per serving: Calories 632; Fat 30 g (Saturated 7 g); Cholesterol 54 mg;
Sodium 869 mg; Carbohydrate 49 g; Fiber 5 g; Protein 41 g

# STEAK-PEPPERCORN SALAD

ACTIVE: 30 min **I** TOTAL: 35 min **I** SERVES: 4

LOW-
CALORIE
DINNER

2    8-ounce beef eye round steaks
4    teaspoons dijon mustard
Kosher salt and freshly ground black pepper
3    tablespoons extra-virgin olive oil
8    ounces white mushrooms, halved or quartered
¼    cup grated parmesan cheese, plus more for topping
3    tablespoons low-fat sour cream
2 to 3 teaspoons brined green peppercorns, drained and chopped,
      plus 1 teaspoon brine from the jar
2    large romaine lettuce hearts, chopped
3    stalks celery, sliced
1    cup cherry tomatoes, halved or quartered
2    cups whole-wheat croutons

**1.** Rub the steaks all over with 1 teaspoon mustard and ¼ teaspoon each salt and black pepper. Heat 1 tablespoon olive oil in a large nonstick skillet over medium-high heat. Add the steaks and cook until browned, 5 to 6 minutes per side for medium rare. Transfer to a cutting board. Wipe out the skillet.
**2.** Heat 1 more tablespoon olive oil in the skillet. Add the mushrooms and cook, undisturbed, until golden, about 2 minutes. Season with salt and continue to cook, stirring, until just soft, 3 more minutes.
**3.** Whisk the parmesan, sour cream, 3 tablespoons water, the remaining 1 tablespoon olive oil and 3 teaspoons mustard, the green peppercorns and brine, and ¼ teaspoon each salt and black pepper in a large bowl. Add the mushrooms, lettuce, celery, tomatoes and croutons and toss. Cut the steak into bite-size pieces; add to the bowl and toss. Divide among plates and top with more parmesan.

Per serving: Calories 425; Fat 22 g (Saturated 7 g); Cholesterol 73 mg; Sodium 796 mg; Carbohydrate 20 g; Fiber 3 g; Protein 34 g

## CHILE-RUBBED STEAK WITH CREAMED CORN

ACTIVE: 30 min | TOTAL: 35 min | SERVES: 4

| | |
|---|---|
| 1 | tablespoon ancho chile powder |
| 2 | teaspoons sugar |

Kosher salt and freshly ground pepper

| | |
|---|---|
| 1½ | pounds flank steak |
| 2 | tablespoons extra-virgin olive oil |
| 1 | white onion, diced |
| 2 | Cubanelle or banana peppers (or 1 large green bell pepper), seeded and diced |
| 2 | cups frozen corn |
| 1 | 5-ounce can evaporated milk (about ⅔ cup) |
| 3 | scallions, thinly sliced |

Lime wedges, for serving

**1.** Preheat the broiler. Combine the chile powder, sugar and 1 teaspoon each salt and pepper in a small bowl. Brush the steak all over with 1 tablespoon olive oil, then rub the spice blend on both sides. Transfer to a broiler pan; let sit 10 minutes.
**2.** Meanwhile, heat the remaining 1 tablespoon olive oil in a medium saucepan over medium-high heat. Add the onion and peppers and cook, stirring occasionally, until the onion is translucent, about 4 minutes. Add the frozen corn; cook, stirring, 2 minutes. Reduce the heat to medium and add the evaporated milk. Cook until thick and creamy, about 7 minutes. Season with salt and pepper.
**3.** Broil the steak 3 to 4 minutes per side for medium rare. Transfer to a cutting board and let sit 5 to 10 minutes, then slice against the grain. Serve the steak with the creamed corn; sprinkle with the scallions and serve with lime wedges.

Per serving: Calories 452; Fat 22 g (Saturated 8 g); Cholesterol 76 mg; Sodium 633 mg; Carbohydrate 23 g; Fiber 4 g; Protein 40 g

## GRILLED STEAK AND VEGETABLES WITH LEMON-HERB BUTTER

ACTIVE: 25 min I TOTAL: 35 min I SERVES: 4

**LOW-CALORIE DINNER**

1½ pounds beef sirloin steak (about 1 inch thick)
1 large red onion, sliced into ½-inch-thick rings
2 large zucchini or yellow squash, cut diagonally into ¾-inch-thick slices
½ cup barbecue sauce
1 tablespoon chili powder
2 teaspoons Worcestershire sauce
Kosher salt and freshly ground pepper
2 tablespoons unsalted butter, at room temperature
2 tablespoons finely chopped fresh parsley
½ teaspoon grated lemon zest

**1.** Preheat a grill to medium high. Combine the steak, red onion and zucchini in a large bowl. Add the barbecue sauce, chili powder, Worcestershire sauce, ½ teaspoon salt, and pepper to taste; toss to coat. Let stand 5 minutes.
**2.** Meanwhile, mash the butter with the parsley, lemon zest and a pinch of salt in a small bowl; set aside.
**3.** Transfer the steak to the grill and cook 4 to 5 minutes per side for medium rare; remove to a cutting board and let rest. Add the vegetables to the grill and cook, turning occasionally, until crisp-tender and charred in spots, about 8 minutes.
**4.** Cut the steak into 4 pieces. Top each piece with some of the lemon-herb butter. Serve with the grilled vegetables.

Per serving: Calories 326; Fat 13 g (Saturated 6 g); Cholesterol 84 mg; Sodium 613 mg; Carbohydrate 12 g; Fiber 2 g; Protein 39 g

# The Steak Grilling Guide

### TRI-TIP
- thick and fairly lean
- boneless
- best marinated

### HANGER
- strong beefy flavor
- center tendon should be removed
- can be chewy; marinating optional

### STRIP
- also labeled "NY strip" or "top loin"
- lean but tender; marinating optional
- available boneless or bone-in

### RIB-EYE
- well marbled and juicy, but pricey
- available boneless or bone-in
- great with rubs

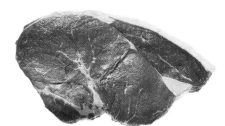

### TOP SIRLOIN
- extra lean
- can be slightly tough
- best marinated

### PORTERHOUSE OR T-BONE
- pricey but super tender
- perfect for sharing
- thick cut; bone-in

### SKIRT
- long, ultra-thin cut
- cooks quickly
- marinating optional

### TOP BLADE
- budget friendly
- can be tough; marinating a must
- connective tissue should be removed

### FLANK
- sometimes labeled "London broil"
- lean, wide cut
- marinating a must

- **Look for marbling.** For a juicy steak, you'll need a bit of fat. Buy steaks with white marbling, tiny lines of fat that run throughout the meat.

- **Avoid prepackaged steak.** Plastic wrap traps moisture, which is no good for steak. Instead of buying the pre-wrapped stuff, shop at the meat counter.

- **Check the grade.** The best steak with the most marbling is labeled "prime." If that's unavailable or too expensive, stick with "choice."

# How to Grill a Steak

1. Make a marinade, if using. (For a basic formula for 4 steaks, whisk 2 tablespoons wine vinegar, 2 teaspoons dijon mustard, ½ teaspoon kosher salt, and pepper to taste.) Marinate the steak in the refrigerator at least 1 hour before grilling.

2. Take the steak out of the refrigerator about 20 minutes before grilling. Remove the steak from the marinade. Pat dry.

3. Preheat the grill. For thick cuts of meat, prepare for indirect heat: For gas, turn off the burners on one side. For charcoal, push the coals to one side. Using tongs, lightly rub the grates with a paper towel soaked in vegetable oil.

4. Season the steak on both sides with salt and pepper just before grilling.

5. Grill the steak, turning, until a thermometer inserted sideways into the thickest part of the meat registers 125° for medium rare. (For thick cuts, sear the steak on the hot side of the grill, then move it to the cooler side to finish cooking.)

6. Transfer to a cutting board and let rest at least 5 to 10 minutes, then slice the steak against the grain—this makes each bite more tender.

# fish&
# seafood

## SALMON WITH CURRIED LENTILS

ACTIVE: 20 min **I** TOTAL: 40 min **I** SERVES: 4

| | |
|---|---|
| 3 | tablespoons extra-virgin olive oil |
| 1 | tablespoon finely chopped peeled ginger |
| 2 | cloves garlic, finely chopped |
| 1 | medium shallot, thinly sliced |
| ¾ | teaspoon curry powder |
| 1½ | teaspoons hot paprika |
| 1 | red bell pepper, chopped |
| ½ | cup red lentils, rinsed |

Kosher salt
Juice of 1 lemon

| | |
|---|---|
| 4 | 6-ounce center-cut salmon fillets |
| 5 | cups baby arugula (about 3 ounces) |

1. Heat 2 tablespoons olive oil in a medium saucepan over medium heat. Add the ginger, garlic, shallot, curry powder and ½ teaspoon paprika; cook, stirring often, until the shallot is soft, about 3 minutes. Add the bell pepper and cook until slightly softened, 2 minutes. Add the lentils, ½ teaspoon salt and 2½ cups water; increase the heat to medium high and bring to a simmer. Partially cover and cook, stirring often and adjusting the heat to maintain a simmer, until the lentils are tender, about 15 minutes. Uncover and simmer until thick, 5 to 10 more minutes. Add lemon juice and salt to taste.
2. Preheat the broiler. Put the salmon on a foil-lined baking sheet, skin-side down. Sprinkle with ½ teaspoon salt and the remaining 1 teaspoon paprika and broil until just cooked through, 6 to 8 minutes.
3. Toss the arugula with the remaining 1 tablespoon olive oil, and salt and lemon juice to taste. Serve with the lentils and salmon.

Per serving: Calories 426; Fat 18 g (Saturated 3 g); Cholesterol 97 mg; Sodium 617 mg; Carbohydrate 21 g; Fiber 5 g; Protein 45 g

# BUFFALO-STYLE SALMON

ACTIVE: 35 min I TOTAL: 35 min I SERVES: 4

2    tablespoons unsalted butter
2    tablespoons hot sauce
1    tablespoon maple syrup
¼    teaspoon paprika
Kosher salt
3    tablespoons crumbled blue cheese
2    tablespoons low-fat plain yogurt
1    tablespoon fresh lemon juice
1    5-ounce package baby arugula
3    stalks celery, thinly sliced
2    carrots, thinly sliced
Vegetable oil, for brushing
4    5-ounce skinless salmon fillets (about 1 inch thick)
Freshly ground pepper

1. Make the sauce: Combine the butter, hot sauce, maple syrup, paprika and a pinch of salt in a small microwave-safe bowl; microwave until the butter melts, about 30 seconds. Whisk to combine. Preheat a grill or grill pan to medium.
2. Whisk the blue cheese, yogurt, lemon juice, 1 tablespoon water, 2 teaspoons of the prepared sauce and ¼ teaspoon salt in a large bowl. Add the arugula, celery and carrots and set aside (do not toss).
3. Brush the grill with vegetable oil. Season the salmon with salt. Grill, brushing occasionally with the sauce, until marked and just cooked through, about 4 minutes per side.
4. Toss the salad and add salt and pepper to taste. Serve with the salmon and the remaining sauce.

Per serving: Calories 410; Fat 27 g (Saturated 9 g); Cholesterol 100 mg; Sodium 420 mg; Carbohydrate 10 g; Fiber 2 g; Protein 32 g

## SALMON-APPLE BURGERS
ACTIVE: 20 min | TOTAL: 30 min | SERVES: 4

1  cup apple cider
2  Golden Delicious apples, peeled and coarsely grated
3  medium shallots (or 1 small red onion), finely chopped
3  tablespoons apple cider vinegar
1  tablespoon curry powder
Kosher salt and freshly ground pepper
¼  cup finely chopped cilantro, plus whole leaves for topping
1¼  pounds skinless salmon fillet, cut into 1-inch chunks
½  cup panko breadcrumbs
2  tablespoons mayonnaise, plus more for topping
2  teaspoons unsalted butter, plus more for the buns
4  potato buns, split and toasted
Potato chips, for serving (optional)

1. Combine the cider, apples, 2 shallots, 2 tablespoons vinegar, 1 teaspoon curry powder, and salt and pepper to taste in a saucepan and bring to a boil. Cook until the liquid evaporates, about 12 minutes; let cool slightly. Stir in 2 tablespoons chopped cilantro.

2. Meanwhile, pulse three-quarters of the salmon in a food processor until finely ground. Add the remaining salmon; pulse until chopped. Transfer to a bowl; stir in the panko, mayonnaise and the remaining shallot, 2 tablespoons cilantro, 1 tablespoon vinegar and 2 teaspoons curry powder. Add salt and pepper. Form into four ½-inch-thick patties.

3. Melt the butter in a large nonstick skillet over medium-high heat. Add the patties and cook until browned and cooked through, 2 to 3 minutes per side. Butter the buns and sandwich with the salmon burgers, mayonnaise, the apple relish and more cilantro. Serve with chips.

Per serving: Calories 584; Fat 25 g (Saturated 5 g); Cholesterol 91 mg; Sodium 598 mg; Carbohydrate 52 g; Fiber 5 g; Protein 36 g

## SOY-MAPLE SALMON

ACTIVE: 20 min I TOTAL: 35 min I SERVES: 4

| | |
|---|---|
| 2 | tablespoons low-sodium soy sauce |
| 2 | tablespoons maple syrup |
| 1 | tablespoon fresh orange juice |
| 3 | cloves garlic, smashed |
| 4 | 5-ounce skinless center-cut salmon fillets (preferably wild) |
| 4 | cups cauliflower florets (from 1 small head) |
| ¼ | cup fat-free low-sodium chicken broth (or use water) |

Cooking spray
Kosher salt and freshly ground pepper

| | |
|---|---|
| 1 | tablespoon extra-virgin olive oil |
| 2 | tablespoons dried cranberries |
| 2 | tablespoons chopped pistachios or almonds |
| 1 | teaspoon grated orange zest |
| 2 | tablespoons chopped fresh parsley |

1. Preheat the oven to 400°. Mix the soy sauce, maple syrup, orange juice, 2 garlic cloves and 2 tablespoons water in a large bowl; add the salmon and turn to coat. Cover and refrigerate 20 minutes.

2. Meanwhile, put the cauliflower and broth in a microwave-safe bowl; cover loosely with plastic wrap and microwave until tender, 6 minutes.

3. Coat a rimmed baking sheet with cooking spray. Drain the fish, season with salt and pepper and place on the prepared baking sheet. Bake until slightly golden around the edges, 8 to 10 minutes.

4. Meanwhile, heat the olive oil and remaining garlic clove in a large skillet over medium-high heat; cook, breaking up the garlic with a spoon, until softened, about 2 minutes. Add the cauliflower and broth, the cranberries, pistachios, orange zest, parsley, ¼ teaspoon salt, and pepper to taste and stir to heat through. Serve with the fish.

Per serving: Calories 392; Fat 21 g (Saturated 4 g); Cholesterol 82 mg; Sodium 527 mg; Carbohydrate 18 g; Fiber 3 g; Protein 32 g

## BAKED TILAPIA WITH TOMATOES AND POTATOES

ACTIVE: 15 min **I** TOTAL: 40 min **I** SERVES: 4

LOW-CALORIE DINNER

1¼  pounds new potatoes, cut into ½-inch pieces
2    tablespoons extra-virgin olive oil
3    teaspoons chopped fresh thyme
Kosher salt and freshly ground pepper
Cooking spray
2    cups cherry tomatoes
¼    cup pitted kalamata olives
2    tablespoons capers, drained
3    cloves garlic, smashed
¼    cup white balsamic vinegar or white wine vinegar
4    6-ounce tilapia fillets

1. Preheat the oven to 400˚. Toss the potatoes with 1 tablespoon olive oil, 1 teaspoon thyme, ¼ teaspoon salt, and pepper to taste in a bowl. Coat a rimmed baking sheet with cooking spray; add the potatoes and spread in an even layer. Roast until browned and crisp, tossing halfway through, about 35 minutes.
2. Meanwhile, toss the tomatoes, olives, capers and garlic with 1 teaspoon olive oil, 2 tablespoons vinegar and 1 teaspoon thyme in a bowl. Coat another baking sheet with cooking spray; add the tomato mixture and spread in an even layer. Roast until softened, 15 minutes.
3. Mix the remaining 2 teaspoons olive oil and 1 teaspoon thyme, 2 tablespoons vinegar, ¼ teaspoon salt, and pepper to taste in a bowl; brush on the fish. Place the fish on top of the roasted tomato mixture and return to the oven until just cooked through, about 10 minutes. Divide among plates and serve with the potatoes.

Per serving: Calories 367; Fat 11 g (Saturated 2 g); Cholesterol 85 mg; Sodium 535 mg; Carbohydrate 29 g; Fiber 4 g; Protein 38 g

## BLACKENED TROUT WITH SPICY KALE

ACTIVE: 30 min **I** TOTAL: 30 min **I** SERVES: 4

| | |
|---|---|
| 2 | tablespoons extra-virgin olive oil |
| 2 | stalks celery, finely chopped |
| 5 | scallions, sliced (white and green parts separated) |
| 2 | cloves garlic, finely chopped |
| 2½ | teaspoons Cajun seasoning |
| 2½ | teaspoons light brown sugar |
| 2 | 15-ounce cans kidney beans, drained and rinsed |
| 1 | 15-ounce can no-salt-added diced tomatoes |
| 3 | cups frozen kale, turnip or mustard greens (about 8 ounces) |

Louisiana-style green hot sauce

4    4-to-5-ounce trout fillets, pin bones removed, patted dry

Lemon wedges, for serving

1. Heat 1 tablespoon olive oil in a medium saucepan over medium-high heat. Add the celery and scallion whites and cook, stirring occasionally, until soft, 4 to 5 minutes. Add the garlic and 1 teaspoon each Cajun seasoning and brown sugar and cook, stirring, 30 seconds. Add the beans, tomatoes and ¾ cup water; bring to a simmer and cook until the liquid is slightly reduced, 10 to 12 minutes. Stir in the kale and cook until tender, about 5 minutes. Add the scallion greens and a few dashes of hot sauce.

2. Meanwhile, mix the remaining 1½ teaspoons each Cajun seasoning and brown sugar and sprinkle on the flesh side of each fish fillet. Heat ½ tablespoon olive oil in a large nonstick skillet over medium-high heat; add 2 fillets, seasoned-side down, and cook, undisturbed, until blackened on the bottom, 3 to 4 minutes. Carefully turn the fillets and cook until opaque, about 1 more minute. Transfer to plates. Repeat with the remaining ½ tablespoon olive oil and 2 fish fillets. Serve with the kale and lemon wedges.

Per serving: Calories 405; Fat 11 g (Saturated 2 g); Cholesterol 94 mg; Sodium 503 mg; Carbohydrate 41 g; Fiber 19 g; Protein 35 g

## ROAST COD WITH ARTICHOKES
ACTIVE: 10 min **I** TOTAL: 40 min **I** SERVES: 4

LOW-
CALORIE
DINNER

1     pound Yukon gold potatoes, thinly sliced
1     9-ounce box frozen artichoke hearts, thawed
½    cup pitted kalamata olives
1     tablespoon fresh rosemary leaves
¼    cup extra-virgin olive oil
Kosher salt and freshly ground pepper
4     6-ounce cod fillets
Juice of ½ lemon, plus wedges for serving
1     tablespoon chopped fresh parsley

**1.** Preheat the oven to 450°. Combine the potato slices, artichokes, olives, rosemary, 2 tablespoons olive oil, 1 teaspoon salt and a few grinds of pepper in a large bowl. Spread the mixture evenly on a parchment-lined baking sheet; bake until the vegetables are tender and lightly browned, about 20 minutes.
**2.** Brush the fish with 1 tablespoon olive oil and season with 1 teaspoon salt and a few grinds of pepper. Remove the baking sheet from the oven and set the fish on top of the vegetables. Return to the oven and continue baking until the fish is opaque and the vegetables are golden brown, about 10 minutes.
**3.** Drizzle the fish with the lemon juice and the remaining 1 tablespoon olive oil. Sprinkle with the parsley and serve with lemon wedges.

Per serving: Calories 373; Fat 17 g (Saturated 2 g); Cholesterol 52 mg; Sodium 1,219 mg; Carbohydrate 24 g; Fiber 5 g; Protein 30 g

## THAI FISH CURRY
ACTIVE: 20 min I TOTAL: 40 min I SERVES: 4

1½    pounds skinless mahi mahi fillets, cut into 1½-inch pieces
2     tablespoons Thai green curry paste
Finely grated zest of 1 lime
1     tablespoon vegetable oil
1     large onion, thinly sliced
2     red bell peppers, thinly sliced
1     jalapeño pepper, thinly sliced (remove seeds for less heat)
Kosher salt
1     20-ounce package cubed peeled butternut squash (about 4 cups)
1     cup light coconut milk (about half of a 14-ounce can)
1     cup chopped fresh cilantro
3     cups cooked rice

1. Rub the fish with 1 tablespoon curry paste and the lime zest in a bowl. Cover and refrigerate while you cook the vegetables.
2. Heat the vegetable oil in a large saucepan over medium-high heat. Add the onion, bell peppers, half of the jalapeño and a pinch of salt. Cook, stirring, until the vegetables are just crisp-tender, about 2 minutes. Add the remaining 1 tablespoon curry paste and cook, stirring, until lightly browned, about 1 minute.
3. Add the squash, coconut milk and 2 cups water to the saucepan and stir to combine. Bring to a boil, then cover, reduce the heat to medium low and simmer until the squash is almost tender, 12 to 15 minutes. Add the fish, cover and simmer until just opaque, about 8 minutes. Stir in the cilantro and season with salt. Serve over rice; top with the remaining jalapeño.

Per serving: Calories 486; Fat 9 g (Saturated 4 g); Cholesterol 124 mg; Sodium 310 mg; Carbohydrate 65 g; Fiber 4 g; Protein 39 g

## TUNA SALAD WITH HERB TOAST

ACTIVE: 20 min **I** TOTAL: 20 min **I** SERVES: 4

| | |
|---|---|
| 6 | tablespoons mayonnaise |
| ½ | cup chopped fresh basil and/or chives |
| Kosher salt and freshly ground pepper | |
| 4 | thick slices crusty bread |
| 2 | tablespoons red wine vinegar |
| 1 | head romaine lettuce, shredded |
| 1 | English cucumber, chopped |
| 1 | 15-ounce can chickpeas, drained and rinsed |
| 1 | pint cherry tomatoes, halved |
| 2 | stalks celery, chopped |
| 3 | tablespoons chopped pickles or cornichons |
| 2 | 5-ounce cans solid white tuna in water, drained |

1. Preheat the broiler. Whisk the mayonnaise, herbs and ½ teaspoon each salt and pepper in a large bowl. Spread ½ tablespoon of the herbed mayonnaise on each slice of bread; transfer to a baking sheet. Broil until the bread is lightly toasted, about 2 minutes.

2. Whisk the vinegar into the remaining herbed mayonnaise. Add the lettuce, cucumber, chickpeas, tomatoes, celery, pickles and tuna and toss to combine; season with salt and pepper. Divide among plates and serve with the toast.

Per serving: Calories 494; Fat 21 g (Saturated 3 g); Cholesterol 37 mg; Sodium 983 mg; Carbohydrate 47 g; Fiber 9 g; Protein 29 g

## SKILLET ORZO WITH TUNA
ACTIVE: 20 min I TOTAL: 30 min I SERVES: 4

| | |
|---|---|
| 2 | tablespoons extra-virgin olive oil |
| 1 | clove garlic, thinly sliced |
| 4 | scallions, thinly sliced |
| 1 | 14-ounce can no-salt-added diced tomatoes |
| ¼ | teaspoon dried oregano |
| 1½ | cups orzo |

Kosher salt and freshly ground pepper
| | |
|---|---|
| 1 | 14-ounce can cannellini beans, drained and rinsed |
| 1 | small green bell pepper, thinly sliced |
| 1 | 5-ounce can solid white tuna packed in water, drained |

Juice of 1 lemon
| | |
|---|---|
| 2 | tablespoons chopped fresh parsley |

1. Heat the olive oil in a large skillet over medium-high heat. Add the garlic and half of the scallions and cook, stirring, 1 minute. Add the tomatoes and oregano and cook, stirring, 3 minutes. Stir in 2½ cups water, the orzo, ½ teaspoon salt, and pepper to taste. Bring to a boil, then reduce the heat to medium low and stir in the beans. Cover and simmer until most of the liquid is absorbed and the orzo is tender, about 10 minutes.
2. Add the bell pepper and continue cooking, covered, until tender, about 3 minutes. Stir in the tuna, lemon juice and parsley. Season with salt and pepper. Top with the remaining scallions.

Per serving: Calories 489; Fat 10 g (Saturated 2 g); Cholesterol 15 mg; Sodium 448 mg; Carbohydrate 75 g; Fiber 8 g; Protein 24 g

## STEAMED CLAMS AND KALE

ACTIVE: 30 min **I** TOTAL: 35 min **I** SERVES: 4

LOW-CALORIE DINNER

| 3 | tablespoons unsalted butter |
|---|---|
| 1 | white onion, halved and thinly sliced |
| 2 | cloves garlic, thinly sliced |
| 1 | tablespoon tomato paste |
| ½ | teaspoon hot Spanish paprika, plus more for sprinkling |
| ¼ | teaspoon dried oregano |
| 1¼ | cups dry white wine |
| 1 | 8-ounce bottle clam juice or 1 cup vegetable broth |
| ¾ | pound small red-skinned potatoes, halved |
| 40 | littleneck clams (3 to 4 pounds), scrubbed |
| 1 | bunch kale (preferably Tuscan kale), leaves roughly chopped |

Crusty bread, for serving (optional)

**1.** Melt 2 tablespoons butter in a large Dutch oven or pot over medium-high heat. Add the onion and garlic and cook, stirring, until slightly softened, about 4 minutes. Stir in the tomato paste, paprika and oregano and cook, stirring, until the mixture begins to brown, about 2 minutes. Add the wine, clam juice and 1 cup water. Bring to a boil and add the potatoes; cook until almost tender, about 8 minutes.

**2.** Add the clams to the pot, cover and cook until they begin to open, about 5 minutes. Stir in the kale and the remaining 1 tablespoon butter. Cover and continue cooking until all of the clams open and the potatoes are tender, 4 to 5 more minutes. (Discard any clams that do not open.)

**3.** Divide the clams, kale and potatoes among bowls using a slotted spoon. Top with the broth and sprinkle with paprika. Serve with bread.

Per serving: Calories 370; Fat 10 g (Saturated 6 g); Cholesterol 74 mg; Sodium 282 mg; Carbohydrate 33 g; Fiber 4 g; Protein 24 g

## FRIED SHRIMP AND OKRA
ACTIVE: 25 min **I** TOTAL: 30 min **I** SERVES: 4

Vegetable oil, for frying
1    cup all-purpose flour
2    large eggs
1½  cups fine cornmeal
2    teaspoons Cajun seasoning
1    teaspoon fresh thyme
3    cups fresh or frozen okra (thawed if frozen)
Kosher salt
24  large shrimp, peeled and deveined (tails intact)
3    large tomatoes, cut into wedges
Tartar sauce and lemon wedges, for serving (optional)

1. Heat 1½ inches of vegetable oil in a medium Dutch oven or heavy-bottomed pot over medium-high heat until a deep-fry thermometer registers 350°.
2. Meanwhile, put the flour in a shallow dish. Lightly beat the eggs with ½ cup water in another shallow dish. Whisk the cornmeal, Cajun seasoning and thyme in a third dish. Dredge the okra in the flour, shaking off the excess. Dip in the beaten eggs, then dredge in the cornmeal mixture. Fry, turning as needed, until golden, about 2 minutes. Drain on paper towels and season with salt.
3. Stir the remaining flour into the remaining cornmeal mixture. Dip the shrimp in the eggs, then dredge in the flour-cornmeal mixture, turning to coat. Fry the shrimp in batches, turning occasionally, until golden, about 3 minutes. Drain on paper towels and season with salt.
4. Season the tomatoes with salt. Serve the shrimp and okra with tartar sauce, lemon wedges and the tomatoes.

Per serving: Calories 476; Fat 27 g (Saturated 4 g); Cholesterol 203 mg; Sodium 516 mg; Carbohydrate 33 g; Fiber 3 g; Protein 27 g

## GREEK SHRIMP AND COUSCOUS
ACTIVE: 30 min I TOTAL: 30 min I SERVES: 4

1    cup whole-wheat couscous
2    tablespoons extra-virgin olive oil
1    pound medium shrimp, peeled and deveined
Pinch of red pepper flakes
2    medium plum tomatoes, diced
1    small bulb fennel, halved, cored and sliced
2    cloves garlic, finely chopped
⅓    cup dry white wine
1    15-ounce can no-salt-added chickpeas, drained and rinsed
2    scallions, sliced
2    tablespoons chopped fresh dill
½    cup crumbled feta cheese (about 2 ounces)

1. Prepare the couscous as the label directs. Cover and keep warm until ready to serve.
2. Meanwhile, heat 1 tablespoon olive oil in a large ovenproof skillet over medium-high heat. Add the shrimp and red pepper flakes and cook, stirring occasionally, until the shrimp are pink, about 3 minutes. Transfer to a plate using a slotted spoon.
3. Preheat the broiler. Heat the remaining 1 tablespoon olive oil in the skillet. Add the tomatoes, fennel and garlic and cook, stirring occasionally, until the vegetables are tender, about 4 minutes. Add the wine and bring to a simmer, then add the chickpeas and ⅓ cup water; cook, stirring occasionally, until the chickpeas are slightly softened, about 3 minutes. Return the shrimp to the skillet and add the scallions and 1 tablespoon dill. Top with the feta, transfer to the broiler and broil until golden, about 2 minutes. Sprinkle with the remaining 1 tablespoon dill. Fluff the couscous with a fork and serve with the shrimp mixture.

Per serving: Calories 481; Fat 14 g (Saturated 3 g); Cholesterol 185 mg; Sodium 392 mg; Carbohydrate 51 g; Fiber 10 g; Protein 36 g

## SHRIMP FRANCESE
ACTIVE: 40 min I TOTAL: 40 min I SERVES: 4

1¼    pounds extra-large shrimp, peeled and deveined (about 20 shrimp)
4    large eggs
Kosher salt and freshly ground pepper
2    tablespoons finely chopped fresh parsley
Pure olive oil, for frying
1½    cups all-purpose flour
⅔    cup low-sodium chicken broth
¾    cup dry white wine
Juice of 1½ lemons
1    cup cherry tomatoes, halved
4    tablespoons cold unsalted butter, cut into small pieces
2    5-ounce packages baby spinach

1. Butterfly the shrimp: Make a deep cut along the outer curved edge, then spread open like a book. Pat dry.
2. Whisk the eggs with 1 teaspoon salt, ½ teaspoon pepper and 1 tablespoon parsley in a bowl. Heat about ⅛ inch olive oil in a large skillet over medium-high heat. Put the flour in a shallow bowl. Working in batches, dredge the shrimp in the flour, dip in the egg mixture and add to the skillet cut-side down; fry, turning, until lightly browned, about 3 minutes. Transfer to paper towels to drain.
3. Pour out any oil from the skillet and wipe clean. Add the broth, wine and lemon juice and bring to a boil over medium-high heat. Add the tomatoes and cook until the sauce is slightly reduced, 4 minutes. Push the tomatoes to one side; whisk in the butter a few pieces at a time. Stir in the shrimp and the remaining 1 tablespoon parsley.
4. Meanwhile, put the spinach in a microwave-safe bowl, sprinkle with water and season with salt and pepper. Cover with plastic wrap and pierce the plastic; microwave until wilted, 3 to 5 minutes. Divide the spinach and shrimp mixture among plates and top with the sauce.

Per serving: Calories 631; Fat 36 g (Saturated 12 g); Cholesterol 459 mg;
Sodium 928 mg; Carbohydrate 36 g; Fiber 5 g; Protein 34 g

## RICE NOODLE–SHRIMP SALAD

ACTIVE: 25 min | TOTAL: 35 min | SERVES: 4

| | |
|---|---|
| 8 | ounces vermicelli rice noodles |
| ¼ | cup plus 2 teaspoons fish sauce |
| 2 | limes (1 zested, both juiced) |
| 3 | tablespoons vegetable oil |
| ½ | jalapeño pepper, thinly sliced (remove seeds for less heat) |
| 1 | tablespoon sugar |
| 2 | cloves garlic, grated |
| 1 | pound large shrimp, peeled and deveined |
| 1 | romaine lettuce heart, thinly sliced |
| 2 | medium carrots, coarsely grated |
| 2½ | cups mixed chopped herbs, such as cilantro, basil and mint |
| 1 | cup bean sprouts |

1. Cook the rice noodles as the label directs; drain and rinse under cold water to cool, then snip into smaller pieces with kitchen shears.
2. Meanwhile, make the dressing: Whisk ¼ cup fish sauce, the juice of 1 lime, 2 tablespoons vegetable oil, the jalapeño, sugar, half of the garlic and ½ cup water in a small bowl; set aside.
3. Preheat a grill or grill pan to medium high. Combine the zest and juice of the remaining lime and the remaining garlic, 1 tablespoon vegetable oil and 2 teaspoons fish sauce in a medium bowl. Add the shrimp and toss to coat. Grill the shrimp until lightly charred and opaque, about 2 minutes per side.
4. Toss the noodles, romaine, carrots, herbs and bean sprouts in a large bowl. Gradually add enough of the dressing to coat; toss. Divide among bowls and top with the shrimp. Drizzle with the dressing.

Per serving: Calories 475; Fat 13 g (Saturated 2 g); Cholesterol 172 mg; Sodium 1,938 mg; Carbohydrate 60 g; Fiber 4 g; Protein 29 g

## SPANISH SHRIMP AND RICE

ACTIVE: 30 min **I** TOTAL: 40 min **I** SERVES: 4

3    tablespoons vegetable oil
1    small onion, chopped
2    cloves garlic, chopped
½    teaspoon turmeric
1    medium tomato, chopped
1    small carrot, diced
½    red bell pepper, diced
Kosher salt and freshly ground pepper
1    pound large shrimp, peeled and deveined
1½  cups converted white rice
1    tablespoon chopped fresh parsley
½    cup frozen peas, thawed
Hot sauce, for serving (optional)

1. Heat the vegetable oil in a large, deep skillet over medium heat. Add the onion, garlic and turmeric and cook until the onion is slightly softened, about 3 minutes. Add the tomato, carrot and bell pepper and cook, stirring occasionally, until tender, about 5 minutes. Sprinkle with ¾ teaspoon salt, and pepper to taste.

2. Add the shrimp and cook, stirring occasionally, until they begin to turn pink, about 1 minute. Add the rice, 2 cups water and ½ tablespoon parsley; bring to a boil. Reduce the heat to medium low, cover and simmer until the rice is tender, 15 to 20 minutes. Remove from the heat and sprinkle in the peas and the remaining ½ tablespoon parsley. Cover and let stand 5 minutes.

3. Fluff the rice mixture with a fork and incorporate the peas and parsley. Season with salt and pepper. Serve with hot sauce.

Per serving: Calories 511; Fat 13 g (Saturated 2 g); Cholesterol 172 mg; Sodium 556 mg; Carbohydrate 67 g; Fiber 2 g; Protein 31 g

## GRILLED BEER-AND-BUTTER SHRIMP WITH POTATOES

ACTIVE: 25 min **I** TOTAL: 35 min **I** SERVES: 4

1½   pounds small potatoes, halved
1     medium red onion, cut into wedges
3     tablespoons unsalted butter, cut into pieces
Kosher salt
1     12-ounce bottle lager beer
1½   pounds large shrimp, peeled and deveined (tails left on)
¾    teaspoon Old Bay Seasoning
¼    cup chopped fresh parsley

1. Preheat a grill to medium high. Stack 2 large sheets of heavy-duty foil; spread the potatoes and onion wedges in the center. Fold up the sides to form a bowl shape. Dot the vegetables with 2 tablespoons butter and sprinkle with ½ teaspoon salt; pour in about two-thirds of the beer. Lay another large sheet of foil on top; crimp the edges to seal.
2. Set the foil packet on the grill; cover and cook until the potatoes are fork-tender, 20 to 25 minutes.
3. Meanwhile, stack 2 more large sheets of foil and spread the shrimp in the center. Fold up the sides to form a bowl shape. Dot the shrimp with the remaining 1 tablespoon butter, sprinkle with the Old Bay and pour in the remaining beer. Top with another sheet of foil; crimp the edges to seal.
4. When the vegetables are almost done, add the shrimp foil packet to the grill; cover and cook until the shrimp are pink, 6 to 8 minutes. Sprinkle the vegetables with the parsley, and salt to taste. Serve with the shrimp and the cooking liquid from the packets.

Per serving: Calories 418; Fat 12 g (Saturated 6 g); Cholesterol 283 mg; Sodium 526 mg; Carbohydrate 33 g; Fiber 4 g; Protein 38 g

LOW-CALORIE DINNER

# COCKTAIL Hour

### STEAMED SHRIMP

Bring 2 inches of water to a boil in a large pot fitted with a steamer basket. Add 1¼ pounds peeled and deveined large shrimp (tails intact), cover and steam until just opaque, 2 to 4 minutes (they'll finish cooking after you remove them from the heat). Spread out on a platter and refrigerate until cold, or up to 4 hours. Serve with your choice of sauce.

## CHIPOTLE COCKTAIL SAUCE

Mix ⅔ cup **ketchup,** 3 tablespoons **horseradish,** 2 teaspoons finely grated **shallot,** 1 to 1½ teaspoons **chipotle hot sauce,** 1 teaspoon **apple cider vinegar** and ¼ teaspoon **Worcestershire sauce** in a bowl; season with **salt** and **pepper.** Refrigerate at least 1 hour before serving.

## CHAMPAGNE-SHALLOT VINAIGRETTE

Whisk ⅓ cup **champagne vinegar,** ⅓ cup **olive oil** and 2 tablespoons minced **shallots** in a bowl. Lightly crush 1 teaspoon **pink peppercorns** with the flat side of a knife; add to the vinaigrette and season with **salt.**

## MUSTARD CREAM

Mix ⅔ cup **mayonnaise,** ¼ cup **heavy cream,** 1 tablespoon **lemon juice,** 1 tablespoon **mustard powder,** 1 tablespoon **whole-grain mustard** and ¼ teaspoon **Worcestershire sauce** in a bowl; season with **salt** and **pepper.** Refrigerate at least 1 hour before serving.

## SOY-GINGER SAUCE

Mix ⅓ cup low-sodium **soy sauce,** 3 tablespoons finely chopped **cilantro,** 1 minced **scallion,** the juice of 1 **lemon** and 1 **lime,** 1 tablespoon finely grated **ginger,** ¼ teaspoon finely grated **garlic,** 1 teaspoon **sesame oil,** ¼ teaspoon **sugar** and 3 tablespoons water in a bowl. Refrigerate at least 1 hour before serving.

## SALSA VERDE

Cook 3 tablespoons **olive oil,** 3 whole **garlic** cloves and ½ teaspoon each **red pepper flakes** and **kosher salt** in a small skillet over medium heat until the garlic is just golden; let cool. Puree with 1 cup fresh **parsley,** ½ cup fresh **basil,** 2 teaspoons chopped **oregano** and 1½ tablespoons **red wine vinegar** until almost smooth. Season with salt.

# pasta & grains

# BUCATINI WITH OLIVE-CAPER SAUCE

ACTIVE: 25 min **I** TOTAL: 25 min **I** SERVES: 4

DONE IN
25
MINUTES

Kosher salt
12   ounces bucatini or spaghetti
1     small clove garlic
2     tablespoons capers, drained and rinsed
Pinch of red pepper flakes
2     tablespoons extra-virgin olive oil
1     pound tomatoes, diced
⅔   cup pitted kalamata or niçoise olives, chopped
3     tablespoons unsalted butter, cut into pieces, at room temperature
3     tablespoons chopped fresh basil
8     ounces fresh mozzarella cheese, finely chopped

**1.** Bring a large pot of salted water to a boil. Add the pasta and cook as the label directs. Reserve ½ cup cooking water, then drain the pasta.

**2.** Meanwhile, pile the garlic, 1 tablespoon capers and the red pepper flakes on a cutting board; mince, then mash with the flat side of a chef's knife to make a paste. Transfer the mixture to a large bowl and add the olive oil, tomatoes, olives, the remaining 1 tablespoon capers and the butter. Stir in the basil and cheese.

**3.** Add the pasta to the bowl with the tomato mixture and toss until the butter is melted, adding the reserved cooking water to moisten, if needed. Season with salt.

Per serving: Calories 660; Fat 32 g (Saturated 15 g); Cholesterol 63 mg; Sodium 453 mg; Carbohydrate 71 g; Fiber 5 g; Protein 25 g

## PASTA WITH TURKEY MEATBALLS

ACTIVE: 25 min **I** TOTAL: 30 min **I** SERVES: 4

Kosher salt
12    ounces orecchiette pasta
2    bunches broccolini, cut into bite-size pieces
8    ounces sweet Italian turkey sausage, casings removed
¼    cup extra-virgin olive oil, plus more for drizzling
4    cloves garlic, thinly sliced
Pinch of red pepper flakes
1    large egg
Freshly ground pepper
½    cup grated ricotta salata or parmesan cheese (about 2 ounces)

1. Bring a large pot of salted water to a boil. Add the pasta and cook as the label directs, adding the broccolini during the last 2 minutes of cooking. Reserve 1 cup cooking water, then drain the pasta and broccolini.
2. Meanwhile, roll the sausage meat into about 20 small meatballs. Heat 1 tablespoon olive oil in a large skillet over medium-high heat. Add the meatballs and cook, turning occasionally, until browned and cooked through, 5 to 6 minutes. Drain on paper towels.
3. Pour off any drippings from the skillet, then add the remaining 3 tablespoons olive oil, the garlic, red pepper flakes and ½ teaspoon salt. Cook over medium heat, stirring, 1 minute. Add the pasta, broccolini and meatballs. Whisk the egg with the reserved cooking water in a small bowl, then add to the skillet and stir until the sauce thickens slightly. Season with salt and pepper.
4. Divide the pasta among bowls. Sprinkle with the cheese and drizzle with olive oil.

Per serving: Calories 613; Fat 25 g (Saturated 6 g); Cholesterol 102 mg;
Sodium 749 mg; Carbohydrate 69 g; Fiber 4 g; Protein 29 g

## HAM-AND-CHEESE NOODLE SALAD
ACTIVE: 20 min I TOTAL: 25 min I SERVES: 4

**DONE IN 25 MINUTES**

Kosher salt
12    ounces multigrain spaghetti
3     tablespoons red wine vinegar
2     tablespoons low-fat plain yogurt
2     teaspoons dijon mustard
2     scallions, thinly sliced
1     tablespoon chopped fresh dill (optional)
Freshly ground pepper
3     tablespoons extra-virgin olive oil
1     green bell pepper, thinly sliced
2     ounces deli-sliced ham, cut into strips
2     ounces cheddar cheese, cut into sticks
½     small head romaine lettuce, thinly sliced

**1.** Bring a large pot of salted water to a boil. Add the spaghetti and cook as the label directs. Drain and rinse under cold water until cool.
**2.** Whisk the vinegar, yogurt, mustard, scallions, dill, ½ teaspoon salt, and pepper to taste in a large bowl. Drizzle in the olive oil, whisking to combine. Add the spaghetti, bell pepper, ham, cheese and romaine; toss to combine.

Per serving: Calories 477; Fat 17 g (Saturated 5 g); Cholesterol 21 mg; Sodium 561 mg; Carbohydrate 66 g; Fiber 11 g; Protein 19 g

## ROASTED VEGETABLE PASTA

ACTIVE: 30 min I TOTAL: 40 min I SERVES: 4

COVER RECIPE

Kosher salt
2   small zucchini, halved lengthwise and sliced ½ inch thick
1   bunch asparagus, trimmed and cut into 2-inch pieces
3   tablespoons extra-virgin olive oil
Freshly ground pepper
1   small onion, diced
2   cloves garlic, thinly sliced
1   28-ounce can diced tomatoes
½   cup grated pecorino romano or parmesan cheese, plus more for topping
9   ounces fresh linguine
½   cup chopped fresh basil

1. Preheat the oven to 425˚. Bring a large pot of salted water to a boil.
2. Meanwhile, toss the zucchini and asparagus with 1½ tablespoons olive oil on a rimmed baking sheet; season with salt and pepper. Roast until tender, about 20 minutes.
3. Heat the remaining 1½ tablespoons olive oil in a large skillet over medium heat. Add the onion; cook, stirring occasionally, until softened, about 8 minutes. Add the garlic and cook 30 more seconds. Increase the heat to medium high, add the tomatoes and simmer, stirring occasionally, 15 minutes. Remove from the heat and stir in the cheese.
4. Meanwhile, add the linguine to the boiling water and cook as the label directs. Reserve ½ cup cooking water, then drain the pasta and add to the skillet with the sauce. Add the roasted vegetables and the reserved cooking water; toss to combine, then stir in the basil. Divide among bowls and top with more cheese.

Per serving: Calories 456; Fat 17 g (Saturated 5 g); Cholesterol 15 mg;
Sodium 341 mg; Carbohydrate 60 g; Fiber 6 g; Protein 18 g

DONE IN
25
MINUTES

# SHAVED SQUASH AND TOMATO PASTA

ACTIVE: 20 min I TOTAL: 25 min I SERVES: 4

Kosher salt
12   ounces mezzi rigatoni or other short pasta
1   clove garlic
1   small yellow squash
2   pounds assorted heirloom tomatoes, chopped
¼   cup extra-virgin olive oil, plus more for drizzling
1   bunch basil, leaves chopped
Freshly ground pepper
¼   cup grated grana padano or parmesan cheese, plus more for topping
4   ounces fresh mozzarella (regular or smoked), roughly chopped

1. Bring a large pot of salted water to a boil. Add the pasta and garlic and cook as the pasta label directs; reserve 1 cup of the cooking water, then drain.
2. Meanwhile, thinly slice the squash on the wide side of a box grater (or use a mandoline). Combine the squash, tomatoes, olive oil and basil in a large bowl; add 1 teaspoon salt, and pepper to taste.
3. Mash the cooked garlic with the flat side of a chef's knife; add it to the bowl along with the pasta, grana padano and mozzarella. Toss until combined, adding the reserved pasta water as needed to moisten. Season with salt and pepper. Divide among bowls; drizzle with olive oil and top with more grana padano.

Per serving: Calories 698; Fat 33 g (Saturated 10 g); Cholesterol 40 mg; Sodium 766 mg; Carbohydrate 77 g; Fiber 7 g; Protein 25 g

## SPAGHETTI WITH PANCETTA AND CHICKPEAS

ACTIVE: 30 min **I** TOTAL: 30 min **I** SERVES: 4

Kosher salt
12      ounces spaghetti
3       ounces pancetta, diced
¼       cup extra-virgin olive oil, plus more for drizzling
5       cloves garlic, thinly sliced
1       red jalapeño pepper, seeded and thinly sliced
1       15-ounce can chickpeas, drained and rinsed
1       bunch parsley, roughly chopped (about 1 cup loosely packed)
Freshly ground pepper
½       cup grated parmesan or grana padano cheese (about 2 ounces),
        plus more for topping

**1.** Bring a large pot of salted water to a boil. Add the pasta and cook as the label directs. Reserve 1 cup cooking water, then drain the pasta.
**2.** Meanwhile, cook the pancetta in a large skillet over medium-high heat, stirring occasionally, until crisp, about 6 minutes. Remove with a slotted spoon and drain on paper towels.
**3.** Add the olive oil, garlic and jalapeño to the skillet with the pancetta drippings and cook until the garlic softens, about 1 minute. Add the chickpeas and cook, lightly smashing them with the back of a spoon, until slightly golden, about 4 minutes. Stir in the parsley and season with salt and pepper.
**4.** Add the pasta, pancetta and parmesan to the skillet along with the reserved cooking water; toss to combine. Season with salt and pepper. Divide among bowls, drizzle with more olive oil and top with more parmesan.

Per serving: Calories 743; Fat 33 g (Saturated 10 g); Cholesterol 42 mg;
Sodium 370 mg; Carbohydrate 83 g; Fiber 8 g; Protein 27 g

## RATATOUILLE PASTA
ACTIVE: 30 min  I  TOTAL: 40 min  I  SERVES: 4

Kosher salt
12   ounces lasagnette or other long ribbon pasta
3   cloves garlic, thinly sliced
3 to 4 large tomatoes, halved crosswise and cored
½   teaspoon red pepper flakes
⅓   cup extra-virgin olive oil, plus more for brushing
1   bell pepper (any color), cut into 8 strips
2   small zucchini, sliced lengthwise ½ inch thick
1   Japanese eggplant, sliced lengthwise ½ inch thick
¾   cup fresh basil and/or parsley, chopped, plus more for topping
2   ounces goat cheese, crumbled

1. Bring a large pot of salted water to a boil. Add the pasta and cook as the label directs. Reserve 1 cup of the cooking water; drain the pasta.
2. Meanwhile, heat a grill pan over high heat. Stuff the garlic slices into the cut sides of each tomato, then sprinkle with the red pepper flakes, and salt to taste; drizzle with 2 tablespoons olive oil. Grill the tomatoes and pepper strips, skin-side down, until charred and tender, about 10 minutes; transfer to a cutting board.
3. Brush the zucchini and eggplant slices lightly with olive oil; season with salt. Grill until marked and tender, about 5 minutes per side. Roughly chop the tomatoes and transfer to a large pot; cook over medium-high heat, 3 minutes. Roughly chop the remaining grilled vegetables and add to the pot along with the herbs and the remaining olive oil.
4. Add the pasta to the pot and cook, tossing, until heated through, 2 to 3 minutes. Add some of the reserved pasta water to loosen, if needed. Divide among bowls; top with the goat cheese and more herbs.

Per serving: Calories 602; Fat 25 g (Saturated 5 g); Cholesterol 7 mg;
Sodium 76 mg; Carbohydrate 81 g; Fiber 7 g; Protein 18 g

## SPICY PASTA WITH TILAPIA

ACTIVE: 25 min **I** TOTAL: 35 min **I** SERVES: 4

½    pound tilapia fillets, cut into small chunks
2    tablespoons extra-virgin olive oil
3    cloves garlic, chopped
½ to ¾ teaspoon red pepper flakes
½    cup dry white wine
1    28-ounce can San Marzano tomatoes, crushed by hand
½    cup chopped fresh basil, plus more for topping
Kosher salt
10   ounces multigrain spaghetti
2    tablespoons chopped fresh parsley

**1.** Toss the tilapia, 1 tablespoon olive oil, 1 teaspoon of the garlic and ¼ teaspoon red pepper flakes in a medium bowl. Cover and refrigerate.
**2.** Heat the remaining 1 tablespoon olive oil in a large skillet over medium heat. Add the remaining garlic and ¼ to ½ teaspoon red pepper flakes and cook, stirring, until the garlic starts to soften, about 30 seconds. Add the wine and simmer until reduced by half, about 3 minutes. Add the tomatoes, ¼ cup basil and ½ cup water. Bring to a boil and cook, stirring occasionally, until the sauce is slightly thickened, about 12 minutes.
**3.** Meanwhile, bring a large pot of salted water to a boil. Add the pasta and cook as the label directs.
**4.** When the pasta is almost done, add the tilapia to the skillet with the tomato sauce and simmer, stirring gently, until just cooked through, about 3 minutes. Stir in the parsley and the remaining ¼ cup basil; season with salt. Drain the pasta and add it to the sauce. Divide among bowls and top with more basil.

Per serving: Calories 435; Fat 9 g (Saturated 1 g); Cholesterol 28 mg; Sodium 71 mg; Carbohydrate 63 g; Fiber 13 g; Protein 24 g

# BROCCOLI-CHEDDAR OVEN RISOTTO

ACTIVE: 15 min I TOTAL: 35 min I SERVES: 4

| | |
|---|---|
| 4 | cups low-sodium chicken broth |
| 1 | bunch broccoli, cut into small florets |
| 1 | tablespoon extra-virgin olive oil |
| 3 | tablespoons unsalted butter |
| ½ | small onion, finely chopped |
| 1¾ | cups arborio rice |
| ¼ | cup dry white wine |

Kosher salt and freshly ground pepper

| | |
|---|---|
| 1 | cup grated sharp cheddar cheese (about 4 ounces) |

1. Position racks in the upper and lower thirds of the oven and preheat to 425°. Bring the chicken broth to a low simmer in a saucepan. Toss the broccoli with the olive oil on a rimmed baking sheet.

2. Melt 2 tablespoons butter in a large Dutch oven or ovenproof pot over medium-high heat. Add the onion and cook, stirring occasionally, until slightly softened, about 2 minutes. Add the rice and stir to coat. Pour in the wine and cook until evaporated, about 1 minute. Add the hot broth, ¾ teaspoon salt, and pepper to taste; bring to a boil. Cover and set on the bottom oven rack. Place the broccoli on the upper rack. Bake, stirring the rice and broccoli once halfway through cooking, until most of the liquid has been absorbed in the rice and the broccoli is tender, 20 to 25 minutes.

3. Remove the rice and broccoli from the oven. Add ¾ cup hot water, the remaining 1 tablespoon butter and the cheese to the rice and stir until creamy (add a little more hot water to loosen, if necessary). Stir in the broccoli.

Per serving: Calories 432; Fat 23 g (Saturated 12 g); Cholesterol 77 mg; Sodium 686 mg; Carbohydrate 37 g; Fiber 3 g; Protein 17 g

## SKILLET CHICKEN AND RAVIOLI
ACTIVE: 25 min I TOTAL: 30 min I SERVES: 4

Kosher salt
1    9-ounce package small cheese ravioli
2    tablespoons extra-virgin olive oil, plus more for drizzling
1¼   pounds skinless, boneless chicken breasts, cut into chunks
Freshly ground pepper
8    ounces white mushrooms, halved
1    cup halved cherry tomatoes
2    cloves garlic, thinly sliced
2    tablespoons red wine vinegar
⅓    cup low-sodium chicken broth
2    tablespoons grated parmesan cheese
¼    cup chopped fresh parsley, basil or a combination

1. Bring a pot of salted water to a boil. Add the ravioli and cook as the label directs; drain, then drizzle with olive oil and toss.
2. Meanwhile, season the chicken with salt and pepper. Heat 1 tablespoon olive oil in a large nonstick skillet over medium-high heat. Add the chicken; cook, undisturbed, until beginning to brown, about 2 minutes. Continue to cook, stirring, 1 more minute. Transfer to a plate.
3. Heat the remaining 1 tablespoon olive oil in the skillet. Add the mushrooms and cook, undisturbed, until browned in spots, about 2 minutes. Season with salt and continue to cook, stirring, until softened, about 3 more minutes. Stir in the tomatoes, garlic and vinegar and cook until the tomatoes begin to soften, about 2 minutes. Return the chicken to the skillet, then add the ravioli, broth and parmesan; bring to a simmer and cook, stirring occasionally, until the chicken is cooked through, about 4 minutes. Top with the parsley.

Per serving: Calories 457; Fat 17 g (Saturated 5 g); Cholesterol 121 mg; Sodium 537 mg; Carbohydrate 28 g; Fiber 2 g; Protein 44 g

# PIEROGI WITH CURRIED CABBAGE

ACTIVE: 20 min I TOTAL: 35 min I SERVES: 4

½   cup plain low-fat Greek yogurt
2   scallions, chopped
2   tablespoons fresh lime juice
Kosher salt
4   tablespoons unsalted butter
½   teaspoon paprika
2   1-pound packages frozen potato-and-onion pierogi
½   onion, thinly sliced
¾   head cabbage, shredded (about 12 cups)
1½  teaspoons curry powder

1. Preheat the oven to 400°. Combine the yogurt, scallions, lime juice and 3 tablespoons water in a small bowl; season with salt. Refrigerate until ready to serve.
2. Combine 2 tablespoons butter with the paprika in a large microwave-safe bowl; microwave until the butter melts, about 30 seconds. Add the frozen pierogi and toss to coat. Spread the pierogi on a foil-lined baking sheet, transfer to the oven and bake, flipping halfway through, until golden, 20 to 25 minutes.
3. Meanwhile, melt the remaining 2 tablespoons butter in a wide pot over medium-high heat. Add the onion and cook, stirring, until golden brown, about 8 minutes. Add the cabbage, curry powder, ¾ teaspoon salt and a splash of water and cook, stirring occasionally, until the cabbage is tender, about 12 minutes. (Add another splash of water, if necessary.) Season with salt.
4. Divide the cabbage and pierogi among plates; serve with the yogurt sauce.

Per serving: Calories 533; Fat 16 g (Saturated 9 g); Cholesterol 51 mg; Sodium 1,232 mg; Carbohydrate 81 g; Fiber 9 g; Protein 19 g

# RAMEN WITH PORK MEATBALLS

ACTIVE: 35 min I TOTAL: 40 min I SERVES: 4

Kids'
MEAL

| | |
|---|---|
| 2 | tablespoons vegetable oil, plus more for brushing |
| 4 | cloves garlic |
| 1 | 2-inch piece ginger, peeled |
| 1 | bunch scallions, cut into 1-inch pieces |
| 1¼ | cups panko breadcrumbs |
| 3 | tablespoons soy sauce |
| 1 | teaspoon sugar |
| 1 | large egg |
| ½ | pound lean ground pork |
| 1 | 14-ounce can crushed tomatoes |
| 3 | 3-to-5-ounce packages ramen noodles (flavor packets discarded) |

1. Position a rack in the upper third of the oven; preheat to 450°. Brush a baking sheet with vegetable oil. Drop the garlic, ginger and scallions through the feed tube of a food processor with the motor running and pulse until chopped; transfer half of the mixture to a pot. Add the panko, 1 tablespoon soy sauce, ½ teaspoon sugar and the egg to the processor; pulse to combine. Add the pork; pulse until just combined. Form into 20 small balls and arrange on the prepared baking sheet. Bake until firm, 8 to 10 minutes.

2. Meanwhile, add 2 tablespoons vegetable oil to the pot with the garlic mixture. Cook over medium-high heat, stirring, 2 minutes. Add the tomatoes, the remaining 2 tablespoons soy sauce and ½ teaspoon sugar. Cook, stirring, until thickened, 5 minutes. Stir in 1½ cups water. Add the meatballs and reduce the heat to medium low; simmer until cooked through, 8 to 10 more minutes.

3. Soak the ramen in hot water until soft, 4 to 5 minutes; drain. Add to the pot and toss to coat. Divide among bowls.

Per serving: Calories 595; Fat 22 g (Saturated 5 g); Cholesterol 92 mg; Sodium 978 mg; Carbohydrate 75 g; Fiber 8 g; Protein 24 g

## CHEESY MUSHROOM PAPPARDELLE
ACTIVE: 20 min ┃ TOTAL: 35 min ┃ SERVES: 4

Kosher salt
2    tablespoons unsalted butter
4    ounces deli ham or pancetta, diced
1    onion, chopped
2    cloves garlic, minced
Freshly ground pepper
12   ounces button mushrooms, sliced
2    tablespoons all-purpose flour
3    cups whole milk
1    8.8-ounce package pappardelle pasta
½    cup grated havarti cheese (about 2 ounces)
2    tablespoons chopped fresh parsley
6    tablespoons grated parmesan cheese (about 3 ounces)

1. Preheat the broiler. Bring a large pot of salted water to a boil.
2. Meanwhile, melt the butter in a large ovenproof skillet over medium-high heat. Add the ham, onion, garlic and ½ teaspoon each salt and pepper. Cook, stirring occasionally, until the onion is translucent, about 4 minutes. Add the mushrooms; cook until tender, about 5 minutes. Add the flour and cook, stirring, until incorporated, 1 minute.
3. Gradually add the milk to the skillet, stirring until smooth. Bring to a simmer and cook, stirring, until thick and creamy, about 3 minutes; remove from the heat.
4. Add the pasta to the boiling water and cook until al dente, about 4 minutes. Reserve ½ cup of the cooking water, then drain the pasta and add to the skillet with the sauce.
5. Add the havarti, parsley and 3 tablespoons parmesan to the skillet and toss using tongs. If the sauce seems thick, gradually add the reserved cooking water to loosen. Sprinkle with the remaining 3 tablespoons parmesan. Broil until bubbly, about 4 minutes.

Per serving: Calories 573; Fat 22 g (Saturated 13 g); Cholesterol 72 mg; Sodium 873 mg; Carbohydrate 65 g; Fiber 3 g; Protein 28 g

## BAKED GNOCCHI WITH CHICKEN
ACTIVE: 20 min I TOTAL: 40 min I SERVES: 4

1 tablespoon extra-virgin olive oil
8 ounces white mushrooms, sliced (about 4 cups)
Kosher salt and freshly ground pepper
2 tablespoons unsalted butter
2 tablespoons all-purpose flour
1½ cups whole milk
1 cup low-sodium chicken broth
¼ teaspoon freshly grated nutmeg
½ rotisserie chicken, skin removed, meat shredded (about 2 cups)
1 17.5-ounce package potato gnocchi
1½ cups loosely packed baby spinach
¼ cup grated parmesan cheese (about 1 ounce)

1. Position a rack in the upper third of the oven and preheat to 425°.
Heat the olive oil in a deep ovenproof skillet over medium-high heat.
Add the mushrooms, season with salt and pepper and cook, stirring
occasionally, until lightly browned, about 4 minutes. Transfer to a
plate and wipe out the skillet.
2. Melt the butter in the skillet over medium heat; add the flour and
cook, whisking, 3 minutes. Whisk in the milk and chicken broth until
smooth; simmer, whisking constantly, until slightly thickened, about
5 minutes. Whisk in ½ teaspoon salt and the nutmeg.
3. Add the chicken, mushrooms, gnocchi and spinach to the
sauce and stir until coated and the spinach wilts. Sprinkle with the
parmesan, transfer the skillet to the oven and bake until bubbling,
about 20 minutes. Turn on the broiler; broil until lightly browned
on top, about 3 more minutes.

Per serving: Calories 598; Fat 35 g (Saturated 16 g); Cholesterol 177 mg;
Sodium 984 mg; Carbohydrate 32 g; Fiber 2 g; Protein 39 g

## ANGEL HAIR PASTA WITH WALNUT-CARROT SAUCE

ACTIVE: 25 min **I** TOTAL: 30 min **I** SERVES: 4

Kosher salt
10　ounces whole-grain angel hair pasta
2　medium carrots, roughly chopped
⅓　cup walnuts
2　cloves garlic, roughly chopped
½　teaspoon dried oregano
1　teaspoon grated lemon zest
Pinch of red pepper flakes
2　tablespoons extra-virgin olive oil
½　cup golden raisins
½　cup grated pecorino or parmesan cheese (about 2 ounces), plus more for topping
Juice of ½ lemon
3　tablespoons chopped fresh parsley

**1.** Bring a large pot of salted water to a boil. Add the pasta and cook as the label directs. Reserve 1½ cups cooking water, then drain the pasta.
**2.** Meanwhile, put the carrots, walnuts, garlic, oregano, lemon zest, ¼ teaspoon salt and the red pepper flakes in a food processor and pulse until finely chopped.
**3.** Heat the olive oil in a large nonstick skillet over medium-high heat. Add the walnut-carrot mixture and the raisins and cook, stirring frequently, until the carrots soften and begin to brown, about 5 minutes. Add the reserved cooking water and bring to a simmer, then add the pasta, pecorino, lemon juice, parsley, and salt to taste and toss. Divide among bowls and top with more cheese.

Per serving: Calories 564; Fat 22 g (Saturated 6 g); Cholesterol 23 mg; Sodium 541 mg; Carbohydrate 75 g; Fiber 9 g; Protein 21 g

# Mix & Match
# PESTO

## 1 PICK A NUT OR SEED

Toast ⅓ cup in a dry skillet until lightly browned; let cool. Pulse in a food processor until finely ground.

- Pine nuts
- Almonds
- Walnuts
- Cashews
- Pecans
- Hazelnuts
- Pistachios
- Sesame seeds
- Sunflower seeds
- Pepitas (hulled green pumpkin seeds)

## 2 CHOOSE YOUR BASE
Add 3 cups total (choose up to 3).

Basil    Parsley    Cilantro    Mint    Collard greens, chopped

Kale, chopped    Arugula    Watercress    Spinach, chopped    Romaine, chopped

## 3 CHOOSE YOUR SEASONING

Add ½ to 1 teaspoon total of the following ingredients (choose up to 3); add ¼ teaspoon kosher salt and pulse until finely chopped.

- Garlic, chopped
- Lemon zest, grated
- Orange zest, grated
- Red pepper flakes
- Fresh thyme
- Fresh oregano, chopped
- Fresh tarragon, chopped
- Fresh rosemary, chopped

## 4 PICK A CHEESE
Grate ½ cup, add to the food processor and pulse to combine.

- Parmesan
- Asiago
- Grana padano
- Pecorino
- Manchego
- Gruyère
- Aged or smoked gouda
- Aged cheddar

## 5 FINISH THE PESTO

Slowly pour in ½ cup extra-virgin olive oil, pulsing to incorporate. Transfer the pesto to a bowl and stir in ¼ to ½ cup of any of the following (optional). You'll have about 1 cup pesto; use about ½ cup for 1 pound pasta.

Mascarpone

Sun-dried tomatoes, chopped

Olives, pitted and chopped

Roasted red peppers, chopped

Fresh tomatoes, chopped

Ricotta

# side dishes

## SPICED OVEN-FRIED POTATOES

Preheat a rimmed baking sheet in a 450° oven. Cut 3 large **russet potatoes** into wedges and toss with salt and 2 tablespoons **vegetable oil;** arrange cut-side down on the hot baking sheet. Roast until golden brown on the bottom, 30 minutes, then flip and sprinkle with 1 sliced **garlic clove** and 1 teaspoon each **ancho chile powder** and **dried oregano.** Roast 15 more minutes. Serve with **lemon** wedges.

## SPICY WATERCRESS WITH GINGER

Remove the tough stems from 2 bunches **watercress;** wash and dry well, then transfer to a bowl. Heat 3 tablespoons **peanut oil** in a small skillet over high heat until very hot. Add 1 tablespoon chopped peeled **ginger,** 1 minced **garlic clove** and 2 teaspoons **Sriracha** and stir-fry 30 seconds. Carefully stir in 2 tablespoons **rice vinegar.** Pour the warm dressing over the watercress and toss. Season with **salt.**

## WHIPPED PARSNIPS

Peel and chop 1 pound **parsnips** and 1 large **russet potato;** put in a saucepan with 2 **garlic cloves.** Cover with water, add **kosher salt** and bring to a boil; cook until soft, 20 minutes. Reserve ½ cup cooking water, then drain the vegetables and return to the pan. Add the reserved cooking liquid, ⅓ cup **sour cream,** 3 tablespoons **butter,** 1 teaspoon salt, and **nutmeg** to taste. Beat with a mixer until smooth. Season with **pepper.**

## WINTER CAPRESE SALAD

Combine 4 thinly sliced **celery** stalks and 1 cup each **bocconcini** (small mozzarella balls) and halved **cherry tomatoes** in a bowl. Toss with 2 tablespoons each **lemon juice** and **olive oil.** Season with **salt** and **pepper.**

## ROASTED BRUSSELS SPROUTS AND CARROTS

Whisk 2 tablespoons **vegetable oil,** the juice of ½ **lime,** 2 teaspoons **sugar,** 1 minced **garlic clove,** 1 teaspoon **kosher salt** and a pinch of **red pepper flakes.** Toss with 1 pound quartered **Brussels sprouts** and ½ pound sliced **carrots** on a baking sheet. Roast at 450° until tender, about 25 minutes. Toss with the juice of ½ lime, and salt and chopped **mint** to taste.

## CHARD, SQUASH AND TOMATOES

Combine one 14-ounce can no-salt-added diced **tomatoes,** 2 sliced **garlic cloves,** 2 sprigs **thyme,** 2 tablespoons **olive oil** and a pinch of **red pepper flakes** in a large microwave-safe bowl; add 2 cups cubed peeled **butternut squash.** Cover with plastic wrap and pierce the plastic; microwave until the squash is tender, about 15 minutes. Add 1 bunch chopped **Swiss chard** (stems removed) and toss. Cover and microwave 5 more minutes. Top with crumbled **pecorino.**

## SMOKY ROASTED MUSHROOMS

Toss 2 pounds whole mixed **mushrooms,** 1½ tablespoons **olive oil,** and **salt** and **pepper** to taste in a bowl. Spread on a baking sheet and roast at 425˚, stirring a few times, until tender and browned, 30 to 35 minutes. Cook 3 thinly sliced **garlic cloves** and ½ teaspoon **smoked paprika** in butter until soft; toss with the mushrooms. Sprinkle with chopped **parsley** and salt.

## POMEGRANATE-GLAZED SQUASH

Halve and seed 1 **acorn squash;** slice into thin wedges. Toss with **olive oil** and roast at 425°, 20 minutes. Cook 1 cup **pomegranate juice** with ¼ cup **sugar** and ½ teaspoon **kosher salt** in a deep skillet until thickened, 5 minutes. Add the squash and 2 tablespoons each **butter** and **pomegranate seeds;** toss to coat. Sprinkle with torn **mint.**

## CARROT-CASHEW SALAD

Shave 1 pound **carrots** into ribbons with a vegetable peeler; put in a bowl. Puree ½ cup roasted salted **cashews** in a blender with 1 tablespoon each **vegetable oil** and chopped **jalapeño,** 3 tablespoons **lime juice** and ¼ cup water until almost smooth. Toss with the carrots; add 2 tablespoons chopped **cilantro** and season with **salt.** Top with chopped cashews.

## EDAMAME WITH BACON

Cook a 14-ounce bag of frozen **edamame** in boiling salted water, 4 minutes. Drain; run under cold water. Cook 3 slices chopped **bacon** in a skillet until crisp, 8 minutes. Add the edamame; cook over high heat until the pods brown slightly, 3 minutes. Add 2 chopped **scallions;** stir. Toss with the juice of ½ **lemon.**

## TEX-MEX SALAD

Whisk ½ cup **sour cream,** 1 to 2 tablespoons **lime juice,** and ½ teaspoon each **sugar** and **kosher salt** in a large bowl. Toss with ½ head shredded **iceberg lettuce,** and ½ cup each chopped **plum tomato,** chopped **cilantro,** chopped **scallion** and shredded **cheddar.**

## WILTED GREENS WITH BACON

Trim and chop 2 bunches **dandelion greens,** watercress or baby kale. Cook 3 slices chopped **bacon** until crisp; transfer to paper towels using a slotted spoon. Add 1 each sliced **garlic clove** and **shallot** to the drippings; cook, stirring, 1 minute. Add 3 tablespoons **cider vinegar** and 1 tablespoon **sugar;** stir until dissolved. Add the greens in batches, tossing to wilt. Season with **salt** and **pepper;** top with the bacon.

## BUTTERY BEANS WITH ALMONDS

Boil 1 pound each halved **wax beans** and **green beans** in salted water until crisp-tender, 8 minutes; drain. Cook ¼ cup sliced **almonds** in 3 tablespoons melted **butter** until golden, 4 minutes. Remove from the heat; stir in 1 tablespoon **lemon juice.** Toss with the beans and 2 tablespoons chopped **chives.** Season with **salt** and **pepper.**

## HERB-STUFFED ZUCCHINI

Split 2 medium **zucchini** and scoop out the seeds; season with **salt.** Combine ⅓ cup **panko breadcrumbs,** 1 chopped **tomato,** ¼ cup mixed chopped **parsley** and **dill,** 2 tablespoons chopped **walnuts,** 1 minced **garlic clove,** 2 tablespoons **olive oil,** and salt and **pepper** to taste. Spoon into the zucchini; drizzle with olive oil. Bake at 425°, 25 to 30 minutes.

## SPANISH POTATO SALAD

Cook 1½ pounds quartered **red-skinned potatoes** in simmering salted water until tender, 10 to 15 minutes. Drain; cool slightly. Combine ¼ cup each chopped **pimientos, celery** and **green olives,** 2 tablespoons each chopped **parsley, sherry vinegar** and **mayonnaise,** 1 tablespoon each **olive oil** and chopped **shallot** and ¼ teaspoon **smoked paprika.** Toss with the potatoes; season with **salt** and **pepper.**

## MACARONI AND EGG SALAD

Soak ¼ cup minced **red onion** in cold water, 10 minutes; drain. Cook 8 ounces **elbow macaroni** as the label directs; drain and rinse under cold water. Toss the macaroni, onion, 1 chopped **celery stalk,** 1 chopped hard-cooked **egg,** ⅓ cup **mayonnaise,** a pinch of **cayenne pepper,** 1 tablespoon each **olive oil** and **white wine vinegar,** and 3 tablespoons chopped **parsley.** Season with **salt** and **pepper.**

## SPICY WILD RICE WITH MUSHROOMS

Cook 1¼ cups **wild rice blend** as the label directs (discard the flavor packet, if included). Meanwhile, melt 2 tablespoons **butter** in a large skillet over medium-high heat. Add 1 sliced small **shallot,** 1 sliced **jalapeño,** 12 ounces sliced **mixed mushrooms** and ½ teaspoon **kosher salt;** cook, stirring, until tender, about 5 minutes. Fluff the rice and add to the skillet; season with salt. Stir in 3 tablespoons chopped **cilantro.**

### AVOCADO-RADISH SALAD

Soak ¼ cup thinly sliced **red onion** in cold water, 10 minutes; drain. Combine 2 tablespoons **sour cream,** the juice of 1 **lime** and ½ teaspoon **hot sauce** in a bowl. Thinly slice 2 **avocados** and arrange on a platter. Top with 4 thinly sliced **radishes** and the onion. Drizzle with the sour cream dressing and sprinkle with chopped **cilantro** and crumbled **Cotija** or feta cheese.

## ARUGULA WITH GRILLED PLUMS

Halve and pit 3 **plums;** toss with ½ tablespoon **olive oil** and a pinch each of **cinnamon, salt** and **pepper.** Grill over medium-high heat, turning, until softened and charred in spots, about 5 minutes. Cut into wedges; toss with 6 cups **baby arugula,** ¼ cup chopped **chives,** another pinch of cinnamon, ½ tablespoon **lemon juice** and 2 tablespoons olive oil. Season with salt and pepper.

### LEMON-HERB ORZO

Cook 1½ cups **orzo** in boiling salted water until al dente; reserve ¼ cup cooking water, then drain. Toss with 3 tablespoons **butter,** ⅓ cup each chopped **chives, dill** and **parsley,** and the zest of 1 **lemon.** Add the reserved pasta cooking water to loosen, if needed. Season with **salt** and **pepper.**

### GRILLED EGGPLANT SALAD

Slice 1 **eggplant** lengthwise into thirds; toss with 2 tablespoons **olive oil** and ½ teaspoon **kosher salt.** Grill over medium-high heat until tender, 8 minutes per side; coarsely chop. Toss with 1 chopped **tomato,** 1 minced **garlic clove,** 2 tablespoons chopped **basil,** and 1 teaspoon each **red wine vinegar** and chopped **oregano.** Season with **salt** and **pepper** and top with shaved **parmesan.**

## MEXICAN HONEYDEW SALAD

Toss 4 cups cubed **honeydew melon** with 2 tablespoons **lime juice,** 1 teaspoon minced **jalapeño** and ¼ teaspoon each **kosher salt** and **ancho chile powder.** Top with **pepitas,** chopped **cilantro** and crumbled **Cotija cheese.**

## SPAGHETTI SQUASH WITH FETA

Put 2 halved, seeded **spaghetti squash** in a microwave-safe bowl; add ¼ cup water, cover and microwave 16 minutes. Let cool, then scrape into strands with a fork. Heat 2 tablespoons **olive oil** in a skillet over medium heat. Add 2 tablespoons **tomato paste,** ½ teaspoon **dried oregano** and a pinch each of **cinnamon** and **sugar;** cook, stirring, 2 minutes. Add ½ cup water and bring to a simmer; season with **salt.** Add the squash and toss. Top with **feta.**

## FRIED ZUCCHINI

Whisk ½ cup each **flour** and **cornstarch,** ½ teaspoon **kosher salt,** 1 cup water
and 1 **egg** in a bowl. Combine 2 cups **breadcrumbs** and ½ cup grated **pecorino**
in another bowl. Slice 2 large **zucchini** ¼ inch thick; dip in the batter, then
dredge in the breadcrumb mixture. Fry in ½ inch of 350° **vegetable oil** until
golden, 3 minutes per side. Drain on paper towels and season with salt and
**pepper.** Serve with **mayonnaise** mixed with chopped **parsley** and **lemon juice.**

## BARLEY-LEEK PILAF

Sauté 1 sliced **leek** (white and light green parts only) in a pot with **olive oil.** Add 1¼ cups **quick-cooking barley,** 3 tablespoons **golden raisins,** ¾ teaspoon **kosher salt** and 2 cups water; bring to a simmer, then cook over medium-low heat, covered, until tender, 12 minutes. Let stand 5 minutes, then toss with some chopped **basil** and **chives,** the zest and juice of 1 **lemon,** olive oil, and salt and **pepper** to taste.

## STIR-FRIED BROCCOLI WITH CASHEWS

Cut off the florets of 1 bunch **broccoli;** peel and thinly slice the stems. Heat 2 tablespoons **vegetable oil** in a large skillet over medium-high heat; add 4 smashed **garlic cloves** and 4 thin slices **ginger** and stir-fry until just golden, 1 minute. Add the broccoli, ¼ teaspoon **kosher salt** and ½ cup water. Stir-fry until crisp-tender, 4 minutes. Stir in 2 tablespoons **oyster sauce,** a splash of **white vinegar** and some **cashews.**

## GRAPEFUIT AND POPPY SEED SALAD

Whisk 2 tablespoons each **grapefruit juice** and **olive oil,** 1 tablespoon **mayonnaise,** 2 teaspoons **honey mustard,** 1 teaspoon **poppy seeds** and ½ teaspoon **kosher salt.** Toss with 1 chopped **romaine heart** and 1 chopped head **frisée,** some **walnuts, grapefruit** segments and sliced **shallot;** season with salt and **pepper.**

# 50 Salad Dressings

No. 16

No. 17

1. **Classic Vinaigrette** Whisk 2 tablespoons red wine vinegar, 2 teaspoons dijon mustard, ½ teaspoon kosher salt, and pepper to taste. Gradually whisk in ⅓ to ½ cup olive oil.

2. **Shallot–White Wine** Make Classic Vinaigrette (No. 1), replacing the red wine vinegar with white wine vinegar; add 1 minced shallot.

3. **Roasted Garlic** Slice the top off 1 head garlic; drizzle with olive oil, wrap in aluminum foil and roast at 400° until tender, 35 minutes. Cool, then squeeze out the cloves. Make Classic Vinaigrette (No. 1) in a blender, adding the roasted garlic and 3 tablespoons grated parmesan.

4. **Bistro Bacon** Make Classic Vinaigrette (No. 1); add ⅓ cup crumbled blue cheese, 3 slices crumbled cooked bacon and 2 tablespoons chopped chives.

5. **Mediterranean** Make Classic Vinaigrette (No. 1); mash in ½ cup crumbled feta, then whisk in 1 tablespoon chopped parsley, 1 teaspoon dried oregano and 1 diced plum tomato.

6. **Dijon** Whisk 3 tablespoons each dijon mustard and champagne vinegar, ½ teaspoon kosher salt, and pepper to taste. Gradually whisk in ½ cup olive oil.

7. **Spicy Honey-Mustard** Whisk 2 teaspoons each honey and dijon mustard, 2 tablespoons lime juice, and ½ teaspoon each lime zest and kosher salt. Gradually whisk in ¼ cup each olive oil and vegetable oil, then add 2 teaspoons chopped thyme and ½ minced jalapeño.

8. **Mango-Lime** Puree 1 chopped peeled mango, the zest and juice of 1 lime, and 1 teaspoon each dijon mustard, sugar and kosher salt in a blender. Gradually blend in ¼ cup rice vinegar and ½ cup vegetable oil.

9. **Italian** Soak 2 tablespoons minced red onion in cold water, 15 minutes; drain. Pile ½ garlic clove, 2 tablespoons fresh parsley, 1 teaspoon dried oregano and ½ teaspoon kosher salt on a board; chop and mash into a paste. Whisk with 2 tablespoons red wine vinegar and the onion. Gradually whisk in ½ cup olive oil.

10. **Creamy Italian** Blend ¼ cup mayonnaise, 3 tablespoons red wine vinegar, 2 tablespoons each sour cream and olive oil, 1 teaspoon Italian seasoning, 1 garlic clove and ¼ teaspoon kosher salt in a blender. Stir in 1 tablespoon chopped parsley.

11. **Lemon Balsamic** Whisk 2 tablespoons balsamic vinegar, 1 tablespoon lemon juice, 2 teaspoons dijon mustard, ½ teaspoon kosher salt, and pepper to taste. Gradually whisk in ½ cup olive oil.

12. **Creamy Balsamic** Make Lemon Balsamic Dressing (No. 11), adding 2 tablespoons mayonnaise and ½ teaspoon each minced garlic and sugar with the vinegar.

13. **Basil-Walnut** Blend ¾ cup olive oil, 3 tablespoons each toasted walnuts and lemon juice, 1 cup fresh basil, 1 garlic clove and 1 teaspoon kosher salt in a blender.

14. **Hazelnut-Herb** Blend 2 tablespoons each dijon mustard and cider vinegar, 1 teaspoon kosher salt, and ⅓ cup each vegetable oil and hazelnut oil in a blender. Add ¼ cup each chopped chives and dill and pulse to combine.

15. **Lemon** Whisk 2 tablespoons lemon juice, 1 tablespoon dijon mustard, 1 teaspoon lemon zest, ½ teaspoon sugar, and salt to taste. Gradually whisk in ¼ cup each olive oil and vegetable oil.

16. **Lemon-Dill** Make Lemon Dressing (No. 15), adding 2 tablespoons chopped dill.

17. **Roasted Red Pepper** Make Lemon Dressing (No. 15) in a blender, adding 1 cup jarred roasted red pepper strips and 1 teaspoon minced rosemary.

18. **Olive** Make Lemon Dressing (No. 15) in a blender, adding ¼ cup pitted kalamata olives and 1½ teaspoons fresh thyme.

19. **Truffle** Whisk 1 tablespoon each dijon mustard and champagne vinegar, 1 minced shallot, ½ teaspoon kosher salt, and pepper to taste. Gradually whisk in ⅓ cup truffle oil and ¼ cup olive oil.

20. **Maple-Walnut** Whisk ¼ cup each mayonnaise and maple syrup, 2 tablespoons cider vinegar, ½ teaspoon kosher salt, and pepper to taste. Add 2 tablespoons chopped toasted walnuts.

21. **Spiced Chutney** Whisk 2 tablespoons each mango chutney and lime juice, and ½ teaspoon each ground cumin and kosher salt. Gradually whisk in ¼ cup vegetable oil.

22. **Chocolate-Balsamic** Blend ¼ cup each balsamic vinegar, olive oil and vegetable oil, 3 tablespoons cocoa powder and 1½ teaspoons sugar in a blender. Season with salt and pepper.

23. **Cuban Mojo** Cook 5 chopped garlic cloves in ⅓ cup olive oil over medium-high heat, 30 seconds; cool. Blend with ¼ cup orange juice, 2 tablespoons lime juice, and ½ teaspoon each ground cumin and kosher salt in a blender. Add 2 tablespoons chopped parsley; pulse to combine.

24. **Ranch** Whisk ½ cup buttermilk, ¼ cup mayonnaise, 2 tablespoons each chopped parsley and chives, 1 tablespoon cider vinegar, ¼ teaspoon kosher salt, a pinch of garlic powder and a dash of hot sauce.

25. **Light Ranch** Whisk ½ cup buttermilk, ¼ cup nonfat Greek yogurt, 2 tablespoons each chopped parsley and chives, 1 tablespoon cider vinegar, ½ teaspoon kosher salt and ¼ teaspoon sugar.

**26. Bacon Ranch** Make Ranch Dressing (No. 24); add 4 slices crumbled cooked bacon.

**27. Smoky Ranch** Whisk ½ cup buttermilk, ¼ cup mayonnaise, the juice of ½ lime, 2 tablespoons each chopped chipotles in adobo sauce and chopped cilantro, ½ teaspoon each honey and kosher salt, and a pinch of garlic powder.

**28. French** Blend ¼ cup each olive oil and water, 3 tablespoons red wine vinegar, 2 tablespoons each tomato paste, ketchup and brown sugar, and ½ teaspoon each paprika and kosher salt in a blender.

**29. Creamy Blue Cheese** Whisk ¼ cup each buttermilk and sour cream, ½ cup crumbled blue cheese, the juice of ½ lemon, and salt and hot sauce to taste.

**30. Buttermilk–Goat Cheese** Pulse ½ cup buttermilk, 3 ounces softened goat cheese, 2 tablespoons white wine vinegar, and 1 tablespoon each olive oil and horseradish in a blender until smooth. Stir in 1 tablespoon each chopped dill and chives.

**31. Caesar** Blend 1 pasteurized egg yolk, 1 garlic clove, the juice of 1 lemon, 1 teaspoon dijon mustard and 4 anchovies in a blender. Gradually blend in ½ cup olive oil and a splash of water. Stir in ½ cup grated parmesan.

**32. Light Caesar** Blend ½ cup nonfat Greek yogurt, 2 tablespoons grated parmesan, 1 tablespoon each olive oil and water, the juice of 1 lemon, 1 garlic clove and 4 anchovies in a blender.

**33. Carrot-Ginger** Cook 1 chopped carrot in boiling water until soft; reserve ½ cup cooking water, then drain. Puree the carrot, reserved water, 2 tablespoons each rice vinegar and chopped peeled ginger, and 1 teaspoon each sugar, soy sauce and sesame oil in a blender. Season with salt.

**34. Creamy Caper-Herb** Whisk 2 tablespoons each mayonnaise, dijon mustard and red wine vinegar, 1 minced shallot, 2 tablespoons chopped capers, 1 tablespoon each minced chives, parsley and tarragon, and ½ teaspoon kosher salt. Gradually whisk in ½ cup olive oil.

**35. Creamy Vegan** Blend 2 teaspoons each dijon mustard and cider vinegar, 1 teaspoon kosher salt, ¼ cup olive oil and ½ cup soft tofu. Stir in ½ cup mixed chopped chives, parsley and chervil.

**36. Creamy Curry** Whisk ⅓ cup each Greek yogurt and mayonnaise, 2 tablespoons lemon juice, 1½ teaspoons roasted curry powder, 1 teaspoon honey and ¼ teaspoon kosher salt.

**37. Orange-Walnut** Whisk 2 tablespoons orange juice, 1 tablespoon sherry vinegar, ½ teaspoon kosher salt, and pepper to taste. Gradually whisk in 3 tablespoons each walnut oil and olive oil.

**38. Thousand Island** Whisk ½ cup mayonnaise, ⅓ cup sweet chili sauce, 2 tablespoons each sweet pickle relish and chopped chives, 1 chopped hard-boiled egg and the juice of ½ lemon.

**39. Green Goddess** Blend ½ cup each mayonnaise, sour cream and fresh parsley, the juice of ½ lemon, 2 chopped scallions, 3 tablespoons chopped tarragon and 3 anchovies in a blender until smooth. Season with salt and pepper.

**40. Red Raspberry** Blend 2 tablespoons raspberry vinegar, 1 chopped shallot, 1 teaspoon each honey and dijon mustard, and ½ teaspoon kosher salt in a blender until smooth. Gradually blend in ⅓ cup olive oil, then add ½ cup raspberries and pulse to combine.

**41. Watermelon-Mint** Puree 2 cups cubed seeded watermelon, ⅓ cup each olive oil and vegetable oil, 3 tablespoons sherry vinegar, ½ teaspoon kosher salt, and pepper to taste in a blender. Add ½ cup torn mint; pulse to combine.

**42. Cucumber-Herb** Make Watermelon-Mint Dressing (No. 41), replacing the watermelon with half a chopped seedless cucumber and the mint with 3 tablespoons chopped dill.

**43. Poppy Seed** Cook ½ tablespoon poppy seeds in a dry skillet, 1 minute; transfer to a bowl. Whisk in 3 tablespoons cider vinegar, 1 tablespoon honey, 1 teaspoon dijon mustard and ½ teaspoon kosher salt. Gradually whisk in ⅓ cup olive oil.

**44. Bourbon-Peach** Puree ½ cup chopped thawed frozen peaches, 1 tablespoon bourbon, 1 teaspoon each dijon mustard and cider vinegar, ½ teaspoon kosher salt and ⅓ cup vegetable oil in a blender. Stir in ¼ cup chopped toasted pecans.

**45. Cajun Scallion** Blend 1 pasteurized egg, 2 teaspoons each Creole mustard and white vinegar, and ½ teaspoon Cajun seasoning in a blender until smooth. Gradually blend in ½ cup vegetable oil. Add ¼ cup chopped scallions and pulse to combine.

**46. Asian Sesame** Whisk 2 tablespoons cider vinegar, 1 tablespoon brown sugar, 1½ teaspoons grated peeled ginger, 3 tablespoons sesame oil, ⅓ cup vegetable oil, ½ teaspoon kosher salt, and pepper to taste.

**47. Miso-Ginger** Blend 1 tablespoon each miso paste and grated peeled ginger, the juice of 2 limes, ½ garlic clove, 1 chopped scallion, 1 teaspoon Sriracha and ½ teaspoon sugar in a blender until smooth. Gradually blend in ½ cup vegetable oil.

**48. Avocado-Wasabi** Puree half an avocado, 1½ teaspoons wasabi paste, 3 tablespoons each rice vinegar and water, and ½ teaspoon kosher salt in a blender. Gradually blend in ¼ cup vegetable oil.

**49. Spicy Thai** Whisk ¼ cup lime juice, 1 tablespoon fish sauce, 1 teaspoon sugar, ½ teaspoon Sriracha and ¼ teaspoon kosher salt. Whisk in ¼ cup vegetable oil.

**50. Peanut-Lime** Blend ¼ cup creamy peanut butter, 3 tablespoons water, the juice of 1 lime, 1 tablespoon each rice vinegar and chopped peeled ginger, and 2 teaspoons each soy sauce and honey in a blender.

No. **30**

No. **12**

No. **33**

# cookies

## LINZER BARS
ACTIVE: 30 min **I** TOTAL: 1 hr 40 min **I** MAKES: about 24 bars

1½ sticks unsalted butter,
    at room temperature,
    plus more for the pan
1 cup blanched hazelnuts
1½ cups plus 1 teaspoon all-purpose flour
⅓ cup confectioners' sugar

½ teaspoon salt
⅓ cup packed light brown sugar
1 teaspoon vanilla extract
½ teaspoon finely grated lemon zest
1 large egg white
¾ cup seedless raspberry jam

**1.** Preheat the oven to 350°. Line a 9-inch-square baking dish with foil, leaving an overhang on 2 sides. Butter the bottom and sides.
**2.** Spread the hazelnuts on a baking sheet and toast in the oven until golden, 8 to 10 minutes. Let cool, then transfer to a food processor and pulse until finely ground. Whisk the ground hazelnuts, 1½ cups flour, the confectioners' sugar and salt in a medium bowl.
**3.** Beat the butter, brown sugar, vanilla and lemon zest in a large bowl with a mixer on medium-high speed until smooth and fluffy, about 3 minutes. Reduce the mixer speed to medium low; add the flour mixture in 2 batches, beating after each, until just incorporated.
**4.** Transfer ½ cup of the dough to a small bowl and stir in the egg white and remaining 1 teaspoon flour to make a smooth batter. Transfer to a pastry bag fitted with a ¼-inch round tip.
**5.** Press the remaining dough into the bottom of the prepared pan. Bake until lightly golden, about 20 minutes. Remove from the oven and spread the raspberry jam on top, leaving a ½-inch border around the edges. Pipe diagonal stripes of batter over the jam, about ½ inch apart. Return to the oven and bake until the stripes are golden brown, 15 to 20 more minutes.
**6.** Loosen the edge of the bars with a knife, then transfer to a rack and let cool completely in the pan. Lift out of the pan using the foil overhang; peel off the foil and cut into bars.

## LEMON-GINGER WAFERS

ACTIVE: 40 min **I** TOTAL: 3 hr **I** MAKES: about 60 cookies

| | | | |
|---|---|---|---|
| 1 | 3-inch piece ginger, peeled | ½ | cup plus ⅓ cup confectioners' sugar |
| 1½ | cups all-purpose flour | 2 | teaspoons finely grated lemon zest |
| 3 | tablespoons cornstarch | 3 | tablespoons fresh lemon juice |
| ¼ | teaspoon salt | 1 | teaspoon vanilla extract |
| 1½ | sticks unsalted butter, at room temperature | | Chopped crystallized ginger, for topping |

**1.** Finely grate the ginger into a fine-mesh sieve set over a bowl. Press with the back of a spoon to squeeze out the juice (you'll need 1 tablespoon juice); set aside. Whisk the flour, cornstarch and salt in a medium bowl.

**2.** Beat the butter and ½ cup confectioners' sugar in a large bowl with a mixer on medium-high speed until light and fluffy, 3 to 5 minutes. Beat in the lemon zest, 2 tablespoons lemon juice, the vanilla and ginger juice. Reduce the mixer speed to low; add the flour mixture and beat until just incorporated.

**3.** Divide the dough between 2 sheets of plastic wrap; form into two 1-by-9-inch logs. Wrap and freeze until firm, about 1 hour.

**4.** Position racks in the upper and lower thirds of the oven and preheat to 350°. Line 2 baking sheets with parchment. Unwrap the logs and slice into ¼-inch-thick rounds; arrange 1 inch apart on the prepared baking sheets. Bake, switching the pans halfway through, until the edges are golden, about 13 minutes. Let cool 5 minutes on the baking sheets, then transfer to racks to cool completely.

**5.** Make the icing: Put the remaining ⅓ cup confectioners' sugar in a bowl; stir in 2 to 3 teaspoons lemon juice, a little at a time, until the icing is spreadable. Spread on the cookies and top with crystallized ginger; let set 30 minutes.

## BLOOD ORANGE MACAROONS

ACTIVE: 40 min I TOTAL: 2 hr I MAKES: about 16 sandwich cookies

1    cup confectioners' sugar
⅔    cup sliced almonds
2    large egg whites, at room temperature
Pinch of salt
Pinch of cream of tartar
3    tablespoons superfine sugar

2 to 3 drops each red and yellow
     food coloring
1    teaspoon finely grated blood
     orange zest
Currant jelly, berry preserves or blood
     orange marmalade, for filling

**1.** Preheat the oven to 325˚ and line 2 baking sheets with parchment paper.
**2.** Combine the confectioners' sugar and almonds in a food processor and pulse until powdery. Sift through a fine-mesh sieve into a bowl, discarding any large pieces.
**3.** Beat the egg whites and salt in a medium bowl with a mixer on medium speed until frothy. Add the cream of tartar and increase the mixer speed to medium high; gradually add the superfine sugar and continue beating until firm peaks form, about 5 minutes. Add the food coloring. Sift the almond mixture into the bowl and add the orange zest. Gently fold with a rubber spatula until the batter slowly drips off the spatula (it will still be thick).
**4.** Transfer the batter to a pastry bag fitted with a ½-inch round tip. Pipe about sixteen 1½-inch circles, 1½ inches apart, onto each prepared baking sheet. Tap the baking sheets against the counter to release any air bubbles, then use a damp finger to smooth any peaks of batter. Let stand at room temperature until shiny and dry, about 15 minutes.
**5.** Bake 1 pan at a time, rotating it halfway through, until the macaroons are slightly crisp and the bottoms release from the parchment, about 10 minutes. Let cool completely on the baking sheets. Sandwich the macaroons with a thin layer of jelly.

## COCOA PALMIERS

ACTIVE: 25 min  |  TOTAL: 1 hr 5 min  |  MAKES: about 24 cookies

| | | | |
|---|---|---|---|
| 4 | tablespoons unsalted butter, at room temperature | 1 | large egg yolk |
| 1 | cup plus 3 tablespoons sugar | 1 | teaspoon ground cinnamon |
| 2 | tablespoons unsweetened cocoa powder | 1 | teaspoon all-purpose flour |
| 2 | tablespoons breadcrumbs | 1 | sheet frozen puff pastry (half of a 17-ounce box), thawed |

**1.** Position racks in the upper and lower thirds of the oven and preheat to 425°. Line 2 baking sheets with parchment paper.

**2.** Pulse the butter, 3 tablespoons sugar, the cocoa powder, breadcrumbs, egg yolk, cinnamon and flour in a food processor until smooth.

**3.** Spread the remaining 1 cup sugar on a clean surface. Unfold the puff pastry and set it on top of the sugar, pressing gently to coat. Flip and coat the other side, then roll out the sheet into a 13-inch square.

**4.** Drop mounds of the cocoa mixture onto the puff pastry and spread in a thin, even layer. Using your fingers, roll 1 side of the pastry into the center, then roll the opposite side into the center to meet it. Trim the short ends with a knife. (If the rolled-up dough is soft, refrigerate until firm.)

**5.** Cut the dough roll crosswise into ½-inch-thick pieces and arrange cut-side down, about 2 inches apart, on the prepared baking sheets. Bake until golden and crisp on the bottom, 4 to 6 minutes; flip with a thin spatula, switch the position of the pans and continue baking until golden on the other side, 4 to 6 more minutes. Let cool 1 minute on the baking sheets, then transfer to racks to cool completely.

## PEANUT BUTTER BROWNIE BITES
ACTIVE: 45 min **I** TOTAL: 1 hr 20 min **I** MAKES: 24 pieces

Cooking spray
1    stick unsalted butter, cut into pieces
4    ounces unsweetened chocolate, chopped
1¼   cups granulated sugar
1    teaspoon vanilla extract
¼    teaspoon salt
2    large eggs

½    cup all-purpose flour
½    cup creamy peanut butter
¼    cup plus 2 tablespoons confectioners' sugar
¼    cup plus 2 tablespoons heavy cream
4    ounces semisweet chocolate, chopped
Coarse gold sugar, for decorating (optional)

**1.** Preheat the oven to 350°. Line a 24-cup mini muffin pan with paper liners; coat with cooking spray. Melt the butter and unsweetened chocolate in a heatproof bowl set over a pot of simmering water, stirring, until smooth. Whisk in the granulated sugar, vanilla and salt until combined; remove the bowl from the pan. Stir in the eggs, one at a time. Add the flour and beat with a wooden spoon until the batter is shiny, about 1 minute.
**2.** Divide the batter among the prepared muffin cups. Bake until a toothpick inserted into the center comes out clean, about 17 minutes.
**3.** Meanwhile, make the filling: Whisk the peanut butter, ¼ cup confectioners' sugar and 2 tablespoons heavy cream in another heatproof bowl set over the pot of simmering water until smooth, about 2 minutes. Transfer to a pastry bag fitted with a small round tip.
**4.** Let the brownies cool 5 minutes in the pan; make an indentation in the center of each with a teaspoon. Pipe the filling into the indentations.
**5.** Make the glaze: Combine the semisweet chocolate and 2 tablespoons cream in a heatproof bowl set over the simmering water. Let sit 3 minutes, then stir until smooth. Stir in the remaining 2 tablespoons confectioners' sugar. Slowly stir in the remaining 2 tablespoons cream until pourable. Spoon over the brownies; top with the coarse sugar. Chill until set, 30 minutes.

## SALTED CARAMEL SHORTBREAD
ACTIVE: 30 min **I** TOTAL: 1 hr 15 min **I** MAKES: about 30 pieces

| | | | |
|---|---|---|---|
| 3 | sticks unsalted butter, plus more for the pan | 3 | tablespoons light corn syrup |
| 1 | cup granulated sugar | 2 | tablespoons heavy cream |
| 2 | teaspoons vanilla extract | 1 | teaspoon instant espresso powder |
| 2½ | cups all-purpose flour | ¼ | teaspoon kosher salt |
| ½ | cup packed light brown sugar | ½ | teaspoon cider vinegar |
| | | | Flaky sea salt, for sprinkling |

**1.** Preheat the oven to 350˚. Butter a 9-by-13-inch baking dish, then line with parchment paper, leaving an overhang on 2 sides; butter the parchment.
**2.** Beat 2½ sticks butter, the granulated sugar and 1 teaspoon vanilla in a large bowl with a mixer on medium-high speed until light and fluffy, 3 to 5 minutes. Reduce the mixer speed to low; add the flour and beat until just incorporated.
**3.** Transfer the dough to the prepared baking dish and set a piece of plastic wrap directly on the surface. Press into an even layer, then peel off the plastic. Bake until golden brown, 30 to 35 minutes. Transfer to a rack to cool slightly, then remove from the pan using the parchment. Cut into triangles.
**4.** Make the caramel: Combine the remaining ½ stick butter, the brown sugar, corn syrup, heavy cream, espresso powder and kosher salt in a small saucepan over medium heat. Cook, stirring occasionally, until a candy thermometer registers 235˚, about 6 minutes. Remove from the heat and stir in the remaining 1 teaspoon vanilla and the vinegar. Let cool 5 minutes, then drizzle over the shortbread. Sprinkle with sea salt.

## PUMPKIN THUMBPRINTS

ACTIVE: 40 min **I** TOTAL: 1 hr 15 min **I** MAKES: about 24 cookies

Cooking spray
1    cup all-purpose flour
½   teaspoon baking powder
½   teaspoon baking soda
½   teaspoon ground cinnamon,
     plus more for dusting
¼   teaspoon ground allspice
¼   teaspoon plus a pinch of salt
½   cup packed light brown sugar
½   cup pumpkin puree

⅓   cup vegetable oil
1    large egg
1    teaspoon vanilla extract
4    ounces cream cheese,
     at room temperature
2    tablespoons unsalted butter,
     at room temperature
½   cup confectioners' sugar
½   teaspoon fresh lemon juice

**1.** Position racks in the upper and lower thirds of the oven; preheat to 375°. Line 2 baking sheets with parchment paper; mist with cooking spray.
**2.** Whisk the flour, baking powder, baking soda, cinnamon, allspice and ¼ teaspoon salt in a medium bowl. Whisk the brown sugar, pumpkin puree, vegetable oil, egg and ½ teaspoon vanilla in a large bowl; add the flour mixture and gently stir with a wooden spoon until just incorporated.
**3.** Drop tablespoonfuls of dough 2 inches apart on the prepared baking sheets. Bake 6 minutes, then remove from the oven and make an indentation in the center of each cookie with the back of a teaspoon. Return to the oven, switching the position of the pans, and bake until set, 4 to 6 more minutes. Let cool 5 minutes on the baking sheets, then transfer to racks to cool completely.
**4.** Make the filling: Beat the cream cheese and butter in a bowl with a mixer on medium-high speed until smooth. Add the confectioners' sugar, lemon juice and the remaining ½ teaspoon vanilla; beat until incorporated. Transfer to a pastry bag fitted with a small round tip; pipe into the indentations. Dust with cinnamon.

## AMARETTO BISCOTTI
ACTIVE: 30 min **I** TOTAL: 2 hr 10 min **I** MAKES: about 30 cookies

| | |
|---|---|
| 2¼ cups all-purpose flour, plus more for dusting | 2 large eggs |
| 2 teaspoons baking powder | 2 tablespoons amaretto liqueur |
| ½ teaspoon ground cinnamon | 1 teaspoon almond extract |
| ½ teaspoon salt | 1 teaspoon vanilla extract |
| 5 tablespoons unsalted butter, at room temperature | 1 cup raw almonds |
| 1 cup sugar | 1 cup chocolate-covered almonds |
| | 2 ounces white chocolate, chopped |
| | 2 ounces semisweet chocolate, chopped |

**1.** Preheat the oven to 350° and line a baking sheet with parchment paper. Whisk the flour, baking powder, cinnamon and salt in a medium bowl. Beat the butter and sugar in a large bowl with a mixer on medium-high speed until light and fluffy, 3 to 5 minutes. Beat in the eggs, liqueur, and almond and vanilla extracts until combined. Reduce the mixer speed to low; add the flour mixture and beat until just incorporated. Fold in the raw and chocolate-covered almonds.

**2.** Dust your hands and the dough with flour; divide in half and shape into two 3-by-12-inch logs on the prepared baking sheet, about 3 inches apart. Bake until puffed and set, about 25 minutes. Let cool 10 minutes on the baking sheet, then transfer to a cutting board.

**3.** Reduce the oven temperature to 250°. Slice the logs crosswise into 1-inch-thick pieces; arrange cut-side down on the baking sheet. Return to the oven and bake, flipping halfway through, until dry and golden, about 45 minutes. Let cool completely on the baking sheet.

**4.** Place the white chocolate and semisweet chocolate in 2 small microwave-safe bowls; microwave in 30-second intervals, stirring after each, until melted. Drizzle on the biscotti; let set 30 minutes.

## CHOCOLATE-ORANGE CRACKLES
ACTIVE: 30 min **I** TOTAL: 3 hr 20 min **I** MAKES: about 48 cookies

2 cups all-purpose flour
2 teaspoons baking powder
¼ teaspoon salt
1 stick unsalted butter, cut into pieces
5 ounces unsweetened chocolate, cut into pieces

2 cups granulated sugar
2 tablespoons Grand Marnier or other orange-flavored liqueur
3 large eggs, lightly beaten
½ cup confectioners' sugar

**1.** Whisk the flour, baking powder and salt in a medium bowl; set aside.
**2.** Heat the butter, chocolate and 1¾ cups granulated sugar in a medium saucepan over low heat, stirring, until melted and smooth. Let cool slightly, then add the Grand Marnier and eggs and stir until combined. Add the flour mixture and stir until just combined. Transfer to a bowl, cover and refrigerate until firm, about 2 hours.
**3.** Position racks in the upper and lower thirds of the oven and preheat to 350°. Line 2 baking sheets with parchment paper. Put the remaining ¼ cup granulated sugar and the confectioners' sugar in 2 separate shallow bowls. Form the dough into 1-inch balls. Add the dough balls, a few at a time, to the granulated sugar and roll to coat, then transfer to the confectioners' sugar and roll to coat. Arrange about 1½ inches apart on the prepared baking sheets.
**4.** Bake, switching the pans halfway through, until the cookies are puffed and cracked, about 12 minutes. Let cool 5 minutes on the baking sheets, then transfer to racks to cool completely.

## GLAZED CIDER COOKIES

ACTIVE: 30 min **I** TOTAL: 2 hr 15 min **I** MAKES: about 24 cookies

| | |
|---|---|
| 1½ cups apple cider | 1 stick unsalted butter, at room temperature |
| 1 cinnamon stick | |
| 4 whole allspice berries | ⅔ cup packed light brown sugar |
| 1½ cups all-purpose flour | 1 large egg |
| ¾ teaspoon ground cinnamon | ⅔ cup confectioners' sugar |
| ½ teaspoon baking powder | Coarse gold sugar, for decorating |
| ¼ teaspoon baking soda | |

**1.** Bring the apple cider, cinnamon stick and allspice to a simmer in a small pot over medium-high heat. Cook until reduced to ¼ cup, about 12 minutes; set aside to cool. Remove the cinnamon stick and allspice berries.

**2.** Whisk the flour, ground cinnamon, baking powder and baking soda in a medium bowl. Beat the butter and brown sugar in a large bowl with a mixer on medium-high speed until light and fluffy, 3 to 5 minutes. Add the egg and half of the cider mixture and beat until combined. Reduce the mixer speed to low; add the flour mixture and beat until just incorporated. Cover with plastic wrap and refrigerate until firm, about 1 hour.

**3.** Position racks in the upper and lower thirds of the oven and preheat to 350°. Line 2 baking sheets with parchment paper. Form the dough into ¾-inch balls and arrange 2 inches apart on the prepared baking sheets. Bake, switching the pans halfway through, until golden brown, 9 to 11 minutes. Let cool 5 minutes on the baking sheets, then transfer to racks to cool completely.

**4.** Make the glaze: Whisk the confectioners' sugar and the remaining cider mixture in a small bowl until smooth. Spread the glaze on the cookies and top with the coarse sugar. Let set 30 minutes.

## CHEWY OATMEAL-CRANBERRY COOKIES

ACTIVE: 40 min I TOTAL: 2 hr 35 min I MAKES: about 24 cookies

| | |
|---|---|
| 1¾ | cups all-purpose flour |
| 1 | teaspoon apple pie spice |
| ¾ | teaspoon baking powder |
| ½ | teaspoon baking soda |
| ½ | teaspoon salt |
| 2 | sticks unsalted butter, at room temperature |
| ¾ | cup packed light brown sugar |
| ¾ | cup granulated sugar |
| 2 | large eggs |
| 1 | tablespoon vanilla extract |
| 2½ | cups rolled oats |
| 1¼ | cups dried cranberries |
| 1 | cup confectioners' sugar |
| 1 | tablespoon milk |

**1.** Whisk the flour, apple pie spice, baking powder, baking soda and salt in a medium bowl; set aside. Beat the butter, brown sugar and granulated sugar in a large bowl with a mixer on medium speed until light and fluffy, about 3 minutes. Reduce the mixer speed to low; beat in the eggs one at a time, then beat in the vanilla. Add the flour mixture and beat until just incorporated. Stir in the oats and cranberries with a wooden spoon. Cover with plastic wrap and refrigerate until firm, at least 1 hour or overnight.
**2.** Position racks in the upper and lower thirds of the oven and preheat to 350°. Line 2 baking sheets with parchment paper. Form the dough into 2-inch balls and arrange 2 inches apart on the prepared baking sheets; press with a spatula to flatten. Bake, switching the pans halfway through, until the cookies are golden but the centers are still soft, 15 to 20 minutes. Slide the cookies from the parchment onto racks to cool completely.
**3.** Make the glaze: Whisk the confectioners' sugar and milk in a medium bowl. Drizzle on the cookies; let set 5 minutes.

## LEMON-ROSEMARY MACAROONS
ACTIVE: 30 min **I** TOTAL: 2½ hr **I** MAKES: about 30 cookies

| | | | |
|---|---|---|---|
| 1 | tablespoon fresh rosemary leaves | ½ | teaspoon vanilla extract |
| ⅓ | cup plus 1 tablespoon sugar | ¼ | teaspoon salt |
| 3 | cups sweetened shredded coconut | 2 | large egg whites |
| 1 | teaspoon finely grated lemon zest | | |

**1.** Pile the rosemary on a cutting board and sprinkle with 1 tablespoon sugar; finely chop, then transfer to a medium bowl. Add the coconut, the remaining ⅓ cup sugar, the lemon zest, vanilla and salt. Use your fingers to rub and toss the mixture until thoroughly combined. Let sit at room temperature, 1 hour.

**2.** Position racks in the upper and lower thirds of the oven and preheat to 325°. Line 2 baking sheets with parchment paper.

**3.** Whisk the egg whites in a medium bowl until frothy. Fold into the coconut mixture with a rubber spatula until combined.

**4.** Drop tablespoonfuls of the mixture about 1 inch apart on the prepared baking sheets. With damp fingers, form each mound into a cone shape. Bake, switching the pans halfway through, until the edges are golden and the macaroons are dry, 16 to 20 minutes. Let cool 10 minutes on the baking sheets, then transfer to a rack to cool completely.

# appendix

# metric charts

## Conversions by Ingredient

A standard cup measure of a dry or solid ingredient will vary in weight depending on the type of ingredient. A standard cup of liquid is the same volume for any type of liquid. Use this chart to convert standard cup measures to grams (weight) or milliliters (volume).

| STANDARD CUP | FINE POWDER (e.g., flour) | GRAIN (e.g., rice) | GRANULAR (e.g., sugar) | LIQUID SOLIDS (e.g., butter) | LIQUID (e.g., milk) |
|---|---|---|---|---|---|
| 1 | 140 g | 150 g | 190 g | 200 g | 240 ml |
| ¾ | 105 g | 113 g | 143 g | 150 g | 180 ml |
| ⅔ | 93 g | 100 g | 125 g | 133 g | 160 ml |
| ½ | 70 g | 75 g | 95 g | 100 g | 120 ml |
| ⅓ | 47 g | 50 g | 63 g | 67 g | 80 ml |
| ¼ | 35 g | 38 g | 48 g | 50 g | 60 ml |
| ⅛ | 18 g | 19 g | 24 g | 25 g | 30 ml |

## Liquid Ingredients

| TEASPOON | TABLESPOON | PINT | QUART | CUP | OUNCE | MILLILITER |
|---|---|---|---|---|---|---|
| ¼ tsp | | | | | | 1 ml |
| ½ tsp | | | | | | 2 ml |
| 1 tsp | | | | | | 5 ml |
| 3 tsp | 1 tbsp | | | | ½ fl oz | 15 ml |
| | 2 tbsp | | | ⅛ cup | 1 fl oz | 30 ml |
| | 4 tbsp | | | ¼ cup | 2 fl oz | 60 ml |
| | 5⅓ tbsp | | | ⅓ cup | 3 fl oz | 80 ml |
| | 8 tbsp | | | ½ cup | 4 fl oz | 120 ml |
| | 10⅔ tbsp | | | ⅔ cup | 5 fl oz | 160 ml |
| | 12 tbsp | | | ¾ cup | 6 fl oz | 180 ml |
| | 16 tbsp | | | 1 cup | 8 fl oz | 240 ml |
| | | 1 pt | | 2 cups | 16 fl oz | 480 ml |
| | | | 1 qt | 4 cups | 32 fl oz | 960 ml |
| | | | | | 33 fl oz | 1,000 ml |

## Cooking/Oven Temperatures

| | FARENHEIT | CELSIUS | GAS MARK |
|---|---|---|---|
| Freeze Water | 32° F | 0° C | |
| Room Temperature | 68° F | 20° C | |
| Boil Water | 212° F | 100° C | |
| Bake | 325° F | 160° C | 3 |
| | 350° F | 180° C | 4 |
| | 375° F | 190° C | 5 |
| | 400° F | 200° C | 6 |
| | 425° F | 220° C | 7 |
| | 450° F | 230° C | 8 |
| Broil | | | Grill |

## Dry Ingredients

| OUNCES | POUNDS | GRAMS |
|---|---|---|
| 1 oz | 1/16 lb | 30 g |
| 4 oz | ¼ lb | 120 g |
| 8 oz | ½ lb | 240 g |
| 12 oz | ¾ lb | 360 g |
| 16 oz | 1 lb | 480 g |

## Length

| INCHES | FEET | YARDS | CENTIMETERS | METERS |
|---|---|---|---|---|
| 1 in | | | 2.5 cm | |
| 6 in | ½ ft | | 15 cm | |
| 12 in | 1 ft | | 30 cm | |
| 36 in | 3 ft | 1 yd | 90 cm | |
| 40 in | | | 100 cm | 1 m |

# index

# C

# Index

# Index

## Food Network Magazine

**Editor in Chief** Maile Carpenter
**Creative Director** Deirdre Koribanick
**Managing Editor** Maria Baugh
**Food Director** Liz Sgroi
**Art Director** Ian Doherty
**Photo Director** Alice Albert
**Deputy Photo Editor** Kathleen E. Bednarek
**Designer** Henry Connell
**Copy Editors** Joy Sanchez, Paula Sevenbergen
**Food Editor** Erica Clark
**Senior Associate Food Editor** Ariana R. Phillips
**Editorial Assistant** Ellery Badcock
**Assistant Photo Editor** Casey Oto
**Assistant Managing Editor**
Heather DiBeneditto

### Food Network Kitchens

**Senior Vice President, Culinary**
Katherine Alford
**Test Kitchen Manager** Claudia Sidoti
**Recipe Developers** Andrea Albin,
Bob Hoebee, Amy Stevenson
**Recipe Developer/Nutritionist**
Leah Trent Hope
**Recipe Tester** Vivian Chan

### Hearst Communications

**Editorial Director** Ellen Levine
**Vice President, Publisher Hearst Books**
Jacqueline Deval
**Creative Director, Content Extensions**
Mark Gompertz
**Product Manager**
T.J. Mancini
**Assistant Managing Editor**
Kim Jaso

ISBN 978-1-936297-71-9

ISSN 2332-0184

10    9    8    7    6    5    4    3    2    1

Published by Hearst Magazines
300 West 57th Street
New York, NY 10019

*Food Network Magazine* and the
*Food Network Magazine* logo are trademarks
of Food Network Magazine, LLC.

foodnetwork.com

Printed in the USA

## Photography Credits

Cover Photograph by Christopher Testani
Food Styling by Jamie Kimm

Antonis Achilleos: pages 32, 35, 43, 80, 84, 91, 108, 111, 124, 132, 147, 164, 186, 197, 202, 231, 236, 240, 243, 247, 259, 268–271

Sang An: pages 116–120

Levi Brown: pages 68–69, 216–217, 294

Kang Kim: pages 178–179

David Malosh: pages 4–5

Charles Masters: page 44

Marko Metzinger/Studio D: page 292

Johnny Miller: pages 36, 40, 55, 56, 83, 99, 128, 171, 210, 261, 263, 303

Kana Okada: page 250

Con Poulos: page 2

Andrew Purcell: pages 278–289

Christopher Testani: pages 16–20, 24, 28, 31, 51, 52, 59–67, 72, 76, 88, 92–96, 100, 107, 112, 131, 135, 136, 140, 143, 152, 156–163, 172, 185, 189–193, 206, 209, 213, 220, 223, 227, 239, 248, 254–260, 263, 267

Justin Walker: pages 23, 27, 39, 48, 75, 79, 87, 103, 104, 115, 127, 139, 144, 148, 151, 155, 167, 168, 175, 176, 182, 194, 198, 201, 205, 214, 224, 228, 232, 235, 244, 262, 264–267, 268, 272–275